I0467688

The Career Whisperer: Behind the podium - A step by step guide to booking speaking engagements

As a public speaker, coach and booking agent for speakers and business professionals for over 30 years, Tony Wilkins has the inside track on what meeting planners look for when booking a speaker. Now Tony brings his experience and resources to his new book **The Career Whisperer: Behind the podium - A step by step guide to booking speaking engagements**. This book is designed to help both new and seasoned speakers find more speaking engagements, book more media appearances and generate more revenue than ever before. "In my career as a speaker, what most speakers generally want to know is the secret to booking more speaking engagements. And so I decided to take my years as a speaker and booker to share my experiences and resources to help other speakers take their careers to the next level. I've spent years interviewing some of the top speakers in the business to gain some insight into how they've made their living as professional story tellers and so this is more than a how to book. It's a look at my journey from telemarketer to author to radio host to magazine publisher to professional speaker and everything in between. It's the lessons I've learned and the people who've helped me get where I am today. "Whether you want to know how to write a one sheet, gain media exposure or learn which events are booking speakers and how to make contact with organizers; **The Career Whisperer: Behind the podium** is your go to book to take you to the next level.

By Tony Wilkins

Tony Wilkins is the host of the Internet sensation Small Business Forum Radio www.blogtalkradio.com/tonywilkins reaching over 150,000 listeners worldwide and broadcasting live every Friday at 3:30 PM Pacific from the historic Payne Mansion in San Francisco. His guests have included famed singer/songwriter Julia Fordham, and San Francisco Mayoral Candidates, Dennis Herrera, Bevan Dufty and Phil Ting. His books include the best- selling Telemarketing Success for small and mid-sized Firms, The Single Person's Cookbook (www.amazon.com) and Surviving the economy-Tips from small business owners from across the globe. His new book, The Career Whisperer is a "how to" series of books designed to help business owners navigate the everyday complexities of running a business. The first book in the trilogy, The Career Whisperer Series: How to double your clientele, increase your sales volume and build your brand through public speaking will focus on the ins and outs of building a business as a professional speaker including tips for doubling your revenue, determining which organizations hire speakers, determining when they hire speakers, learning how to approach event planners and most importantly a comprehensive listing of contact info for decision makers. He has been featured in the media on Channel 7's (ABC) The View from the Bay, Progressive Pulse Magazine, B.A.R (Bay Area Reporter) and the 10% Show. Tony is a much sought after speaker and coach for The SBA(Small Business Administration)The Learning Annex, CIIS (California Institute of Integral Studies), and The Academy of Art College –SF. Mr. Wilkins is also the publisher of Small Business Forum Magazine, Foodie Quarterly, and Podium Magazine. In addition, he is the host of The Tony Wilkins Show on livestream.com and has launched a very successful booking service for authors and speakers. Lastly, he will be writing, producing and directing a new docu-series also titled The Career Whisper, focusing on several speakers at different stages of their careers. The docu series will show their frustrations, their triumphs and journey as they take their careers to the next level.

Acknowledgements

I'd like to thank everyone that helped me get to this point in my life and career. I want to thank those speakers that inspired me to write this book to help other speakers on their journey to success. A special thanks to my family including my girls Leslie and Robyn. My Aunt Orlean for never judging me; even when I was acting like an asshole. Thank you for keeping me grounded. My sister Denise and brother Rob for being there and staying connected. I love you more than I can say. A big kiss to the women in my life both here and waiting for me at the Golden Gates (I'm Southern Baptist so no guarantee I'll make it) particularly my sister Diane, and my two moms Zelma and Annie Mae. Thanks for standing with me through the hard times, I feel your presence. I want to thank my clients and business associates that have stood by me, supported me and encouraged me to do more even when I didn't think I had anything left to give or do. My thanks to Carmen Milagro, Daphne Evans Giovannelli and an extra special thank you to Irv Spivak and George Parrish Kim Angel-wood and Tonya Hofmann for always believing in me. Finally (and if I left anyone out my apologies) a major thank you to my buddy Max because you were there when I needed you. You inspire me, make me laugh and make me think and generally raise the bar on how I do business and live my life.

Tony Wilkins

Contents

Introduction: My journey. My story

I've been a professional speaker for nearly 30 years. And for the most part I've done very well for myself. But the longer I'm in business, the more I learn about what I don't know about professional speaking and more importantly what I don't know about getting paid well to do it. Don't get me wrong, I make a pretty good living as a speaker, coach and small business strategist and have had the opportunity to council business owners on my various areas of expertise on a global level. I've traveled the world and been paid handsomely for my work. But recently I began to realize that I wasn't reaching my full potential as a professional speaker. I was filling rooms but not auditoriums. I was making a good living, but not quite six figures as a speaker. And there were several reasons. Mine is a specialized field (the lie I told myself) and so I'm not likely to sell Tony Robbins-like quantities of tickets to one of my events(at this point); but I felt I was still out there making my way and making a difference. I was content-or so I thought. And then a friend of mine gave me a reality check. Every year I'm asked to teach a workshop during Small Business Week (which has been an honor) for the past 6 years because it meant exposure for my books, radio show etc.) But one year the invitation didn't come (they were booked up that year-they said). And while I was disappointed, I wasn't exactly devastated. That's when my buddy asked me why I was still accepting non-paying gigs like Small Business Week. In her view, accepting speaking gigs like that was for newer-younger-less established business owners and speakers and not for someone as well established as me (Here's a tip. Never accept advice from someone not in the industry- no matter how well meaning). "Isn't accepting a gig like that beneath you" she asked? The truth is that a speaker is only speaking for free if they don't generate sales from the gig or you don't book a second gig from the first one. Still she made an interesting point. I had already established myself as a successful business owner and radio personality" so what's the pay off in accepting gigs that aren't designed to elevate your brand," she said? Her comment got me thinking about the gigs I was actually booking for myself. Were these gigs actually helping me land more speaking opportunities or better ones, with a bigger pay check? The answer was –sort of….. This got me to thinking about ways I can actively find gigs that would not only pay well but also give me the exposure I needed to become the go to person in my field. But how would I go about that? How would I find more high profile speaking opportunities and how do I contact the decision makers and how do other speakers do it? Here's the thing. Getting a paid speaking gig at say Facebook is different from getting one at Joe's Automotive. Not better or worse-just different. Decision makers are easier to reach at smaller firms and pay faster (if not as well) as the larger corporations. And that's when my journey (and a lot of research) began to find more high profile speaking gigs that paid better. This is not about dismissing or rejecting offers to coach smaller accounts or pro bono gigs (because even a no pro bono gig can pay big dividends) but rather elevating my brand, generating more revenue (not to mention working smarter). This book comes from years of research and hundreds of interviews with highly successful professional speakers, coaches, media personalities, authors, consultants, keynote speakers and meeting planners (the people who hire the speakers). I hope these tips help you as well.

Chapter One:Life as an author

I never planned on becoming a public speaker, which is ironic since I'm painfully shy at times and earn the majority of my revenue as a coach and speaker. As a kid I always seemed to come alive whenever I was on stage performing. I remember the adrenaline rush I got when I wrote, produced and directed my first play. I must've been about 10 or so and my teacher allowed me to perform it on stage at a school assembly. Looking back, I wanted that applause which again is ironic since as an adult I tend to shy away from the spotlight. Grade school, followed by several plays in high school and college was how I knew I wanted to be on stage. Stupid me (however) figured that I would go into acting (not public speaking) which would help me get over my shyness.

One of my first teaching gigs came in the form of a request from one of my telemarketing clients (I had started my first firm Telecorp Telemarketing in my early 20's by this point) who was having trouble booking sales meetings with prospects and wanted to know how I did it so effortlessly. Now it's important to note that once again my intention was not to go into telemarketing. By this point I was pretty clear that I wanted to earn my living as a writer (another gift from childhood) because I was still so uncomfortable talking to people. During this time I had no idea what to charge or what my value was(always know your value and get others to pay you accordingly). What I did know was that my expertise had value because the client placed a value on my knowledge. My challenge was to put a dollar amount with that value. So my first paying gig as a coach was a whopping $75.00 an hour; which may seem like a miniscule amount, but when you're in your early 20's and had never made much more than minimum wage which was about $6.00 an hour at the time, then $75 an hour was a gold mine. My main function as a business owner was to close telemarketing accounts. I didn't know how to do anything else(I thought) so I became the highest paid telemarketing consultant in Chicago and one of few Black (if not the only one) owned tm firms.

This was a good time for me. Good money, and somewhat respected in the business community as a telemarketer. A Golden Age. I say somewhat because truth be told no one respects a telemarketer no matter how you dress it up. No matter how much money you make my job was to either sell something over the phone or set an appointment so my client could sell something. When people asked me what I did for a living I always said that I owned a business; which got the attention of the person I was talking to until I told them what type of company it was. Then of course they had to move on to someone else. This of course, got me to thinking about my exit strategy. Now don't get me wrong, I loved owning a company and for the most part loved the work-at first. But luckily I was intuitive enough to know that telemarketing wasn't going to be my life or my way of earning a decent living-long term.

At this time I knew several truths. First, I knew that I didn't want to be a 50 year old telemarketer. Second, I knew that if I was ever going to feel respected by my peers, then I would have to position myself in a way that gave me respectability, money and power. Making cold calls wasn't going to cut it.

And teaching others how to do what I do wasn't going to get me where I wanted to go either although it was a step up). So I came up with the idea of coaching others to do what others were paying me to do. Keep in mind that there was no Internet (it was the 80's folks) and I didn't know enough about launching a full time speaking business to sustain me financially. What I became was a telemarketing consultant; which sounds better than "I'm a telemarketer "or" I'm the owner of a telemarketing firm". And so I became a consultant as who occasionally spoke professionally.

I don't really remember too many details from the first public speaking gig I ever did but I do remember that it was at the SBA(Small Business Administration) in Chicago. I remember being nervous and jittery and long winded. I remember that I felt intimidated by the audience and although I felt it was a disaster, I landed three new clients from that one talk. The lesson for me was that any talk that results in more speaking engagements is a good talk.

The idea for my first book Telemarketing Success came from the fact that so many of my clients at the time were asking me how to do what I do which at the time was setting quality appointments for my B2B customers. Now while most people feel that any idiot can book appointments and telemarket, the truth is that it takes an enormous amount of skill, endurance, mental invulnerability and persistence to deal with all that rejection on a daily basis; which is why I never understand why some business owners only want to pay telemarketers a minimum wage to help them make money. But I digress. I decided that a good way to get my ideas in one place and make it easily accessible to clients would be to write a book.

The evolution of Tony Wilkins

Now as any writer or aspiring author will tell you, writing takes discipline and persistence (much like telemarketing). And while every literary expert will tell you to write every day, the truth of the matter is that most of us really don't have the financial resources or time to devote to writing every day. Life and the paying of bills unfortunately get in the way. And so my first book actually took 10 years to write. Why so long? Think of it this way. If you're in your late 20's and trying to run a business, the time you spend actually going to meetings, managing finances and just every day time management can be daunting(not to mention building a fulfilling personal life). By the time you have time to write you're either too tired or not sure you have anything to write about. Hence the decade long literary journey. These days when I'm writing a new book, I have it down to about a year.

The next hurdle was finding a publisher and an agent. Now I'm not going to get into all the rejection letters, I received along with the negative feedback from friends, family and literary experts (all of whom told me that there was no market for a telemarketing book for small business owners). After submitting multiple manuscripts and queries, I opted for a surefire yet controversial route... self-publication.

Now you have to remember that 10+ years ago self-publishing was frowned upon by, well just about everyone but especially anyone in the literary community. To self-publish your work (at that time) meant that you weren't good enough to publish your work traditionally. It's important to make 2 points here. First back in 2008 the literary community saw a downsizing of the industry resulting in fewer publishing houses, bookstores and literary agencies to handle the sheer volume of literary work. This downsizing resulted in most authors looking for alternative ways to publish their work including e-books, and self-publishing. Second, self-publishing gives the author nearly complete control over their success. For example, with self-publishing, the author has nearly 100% control, in most cases, over the artwork, marketing, and content ,whether they publish through a publishing house like Xlibris.com(which was where I published my first book) or thru Createspace.com (owned by Amazon) which carries my other 3 books. Here's the pros and cons of traditional publishing vs. self-publishing and why it's important to the story…..

The pros and cons of Self-publishing and Traditional publishing

1. Self-publishing gives you almost full control over content, book cover, design, pricing, marketing, distribution. Whereas traditional publishing gives you little or no control over your work. Essentially you are at the whim of the publisher and agent. Also publishing your work on your own gives you the ability to fast track your work and release it to the public in a few months whereas traditional publishing can take up to 18 month minimum.

2. Createspace.com(which is owned by Amazon.com) has self-publishing options without upfront costs. For the most part the service is free. The only thing you pay for is for extras. For example, if you have a special design that you'd like to upload then it may cost you a nominal fee. Traditional publishers and agents handle everything from the design of the cover to the layout to the marketing.

3. Traditional publishing allows you to ask for a decent advance on book sales before the book is even published which gives you some financial cushion (between $3-25,000), but don't expect to get a million dollar advance. It rarely ever happens these days. Self -publishing means you're taking on all the risks.

4. Self-publishing- Editing is up to you. This is where you either have to be a really good editor or spend a few bucks to hire an editor. Createpace also has editing services for a nominal amount. With traditional publisher, an editor is assigned to you.

5. If a self-published work is marketed properly you can create a very steady revenue stream which includes speaking engagements, sponsorships etc. With traditional publishing a publicist is assigned to you to book speaking engagements, media opportunities and book signings.

6. Self- publishing is a lot of work particularly if you're not sure how to get going. This is where it might pay to work with a consultant or self -publishing firm like Xlibris.com. And while it may cost you more money, they can help you craft a platform that works for you. With traditional publishing, you simply write the book and work with people assigned to help you bring it to market. It's still hard work but you at least have a team of experts to work help you.

7. With self- publication you still have to promote it which means it may take a while before you make any money. Again, if your skill isn't in marketing it may pay to hire someone to market your book. With traditional publishing, a marketing agent is assigned to you.

8. Traditional publishing is much harder to break into because the market has become more competitive and saturated than ever. It's no longer enough to have a well written book; it must also be marketable and a clear money maker. Traditional publishers aren't taking the risks they once did with unknown authors-therefore getting a great book published can take years...if ever. This is the primary reason more and more authors are going the self-publishing route.

9. With traditional publishing edits and re-writes are at the discretion of the publisher and can take months. However with self-publishing, edits are at the discretion of the author.

10. Traditional publishers handle the marketing, distribution and, editing which can net a great deal of money for everyone involved but can also mean that your book will look entirely different from your original concept and manuscript.

11. The main reason self -publishing has become so attractive is that authors want to fast track their work. Think of it this way. An unknown author can spend months just trying to get an agent to represent them. Self- publishing sort of takes the guess work out of it.

The bottom line is that regardless of the route you choose, be sure to do your research so that you know the pros and cons of each.

Which way do I go?
So after countless rejections and disappointments from agents and publishers, I opted to self-publish my work thru publishing dynamo Xlibris.com. Deciding to publish this way was in itself a challenge because aside from the financial investment (over $1200) it also meant that my life would change drastically. I understood this on a basic level but had no idea to what extent. Naturally the universe would provide some invaluable lessons to guide me on my journey.

But I'm an author...
Choosing to self-publish my work meant that I would finally see my dream realized. Despite not having gone the traditional route and spending a great deal of money I would finally have my book. Little did I know that my choice would put me on a career path that would be both unexpected and rewarding.

Self-publishing thru Xlibris.com was a great decision because it allowed me the control and freedom to publish my work in a fraction of the time. And even introducing myself as the author of a telemarketing book sounded much better than simply stating that I was a high priced telemarketer. Sept 16th 2004 was an important date because it was the release date of my first book, Telemarketing Success for Small and Mid-size firms-4 days before my 41st birthday. This date was significant because I knew that I would publish my first book before I turned 41 which meant I got it just under the wire of my goal of publishing by age 40. But now the real work would begin.

My first book signing (a few months later) was held at a now defunct high end eatery in San Francisco called Mecca. With a full house, food and wine flowing the inevitable question came my way." Are you going to give any talks to help sell books"? I hadn't really given it too much thought to be honest. I mean I knew I would have to give some talks at some point because after all speaking is how most authors make their living. But I didn't really have a clue how or where to start. And then I got an idea because I'm an author and a speaker…..

Chapter Two: Life as a speaker

With the publication of my first book, Telemarketing Success for Small and Mid-size Firms, I quickly began to realize that in order for anyone to buy my book they first had to know it existed. I theorized that without a marketing budget or publicist behind me I had to find a way to reach my target audience that would not only sell books but generate interest in my consulting work as well. And because I was so new to the industry, I had no clue how to launch a career as a speaker let alone the type of speaker I wanted to be. So I chose the route of least resistance and became a workshop speaker theorizing that teaching workshops was closer to what I wanted to be doing in my career. I mention this because most speakers focus on one aspect or type of speaking. They dream of commanding six figures per speaking gig and flying around in private jets. In other words they want to be keynote speakers, something I knew nothing about. For me, it was about teaching what I knew, selling books and hopefully generating enough interest to land a few paying consulting clients per month. Much of what I'm about to share with you were lessons I learned in my first few years of teaching to sell books. I hope you find the info useful….

How NOT to ruin your first seminar or workshop

So you've finally decided to host your first seminar or workshop. Terrific, Welcome to the start of a whole new career as a paid speaker. And while everyone has useful anecdotes to share; not all of them should be done in a public forum. So here are some common mistakes to help minimize any hiccups that may come up. By the way, these tips are obviously for the novices out there.

1.   Know your audience. Before you can put a seminar or workshop together it's important to understand who you'll be speaking in front of. In a way it's more important to know your audience before choosing your topic. Because the topic can be tweaked based on the audience but it's more difficult to change the audience once the topic has been decided. The mistake that many beginners make is trying to craft a topic based on topics their audience has little or no interest in hearing. It becomes more about teaching the workshop because the speaker is interested rather than teaching a topic attendees are interested in. It's partly why ticket sales for first timers may be low.

2.   Choose your topic. Once you've decided on your audience, decide what you talking points might be of interest to your audience as opposed to what you want to talk about. Why are these talking points of interest to your audience? What message do you want to deliver to your audience? Is the message clear? One reason for low ticket sales is a message that is unclear to the audience. Remember, you may know what points you want to get across but does your audience? Is it interesting to your audience? For example a financial advisor may want to discuss the current Fed rates but that doesn't mean that the audience is interested or cares. However, offering money saving tips on home loans, retirement and the like is always a crowd pleaser.

3.   Choose your location. Is this a webinar? Choose a web hosting service that will accommodate multiple callers. If this is a seminar where you're expected to be physically present (my favorite) then choose a location that's cost effective, in a decent area of the city, easily accessible and has good parking. Most beginners are not rolling in the dough so choose a venue in the $30 an hour range. That way if you charge say $50 per person for a 2 hour seminar with only 10 attendees you've still made a profit of $440. Until you build a name for yourself, don't expect to sell out 100 seat venues. A venue that seats 25 or less is just fine to start.

4.   Name your price. It's just as bad to sell your seminar for too much as it is to sell it for too little. But if you have to choose start with under valuing your seminar at least at first. There's nothing wrong with offering an early bird special. The reason is that it's easier to increase the price once sales start coming in but more difficult to lower after the fact. Doing so sends a message that you can't sell tickets.

5.   Promote like there's no tomorrow. The one mistake newcomers make when hosting their first seminar is under promotion, lack of consistency and having little time to promote the seminar. Personally I like to give myself 90 days to promote any event beginning with a lower price for a limited time; raising the price after a certain amount of time. Offering attendees a discount initially gives them an incentive to buy early before the rate increases and also gives a good indication of turn out as well as whether the talking points are of interest to the audience.

6.   Partner with others to help get the word out. Let's face it, we can't do everything ourselves so it becomes important to partner with others that have as many (if not more) contacts as you do. I tend to partner with BNI groups, associations and anyone that can help to get the word out about my event. My secret weapon? I offer ticket buyers free advertising or other amenities for purchasing a high end ticket. Now to be clear, I'm not giving away the farm but if someone buys a ticket to one of my talks which can cost upwards of $200 isn't it worth it to offer say 4 ads on my radio show as incentive? It's about making money as well as filling seats which can be difficult to do if you're not say, Tony Robbins. This also cross promotes other products/services like my radio show/magazines and entices them to try advertising with me thru special promotions which translates into revenue.

The bottom line is to think ahead. Plan ahead and always have a plan B when things go wrong.

Setting up speaking engagements

Barbara's story

Because I deal with so many different types of speakers, I'll occasionally work with someone that just doesn't get it. The reasons some speak professionally can vary, but whatever the reason, you should have a plan and a purpose. "Barbara" is a perfect example of not having a plan in place (more on her later). Some of these reasons may sound familiar….

I speak because…..

1.   I want to make a living as a speaker

2.   I like the attention

3.   I want to help/inspire others

4.   I want an effective way to get my message out to others

5.   I want to sell my books and services at events where I'm in the spotlight

Whatever your reasons for speaking, part of your goal/reasons should be to earn money and to promote your work. "Barbara", a speaker I represented until recently, was a perfectly pleasant woman, but only interested in speaking with hospital administrators interested in booking her to speak on her area of expertise. Sounds reasonable right? Like most relatively new and unknown speakers she had several obstacles to overcome.

1.   First no one knew who she was so although her one sheet was impressive she was up against other more well- known speakers all vying for the same speaking opportunity; an uphill battle to be sure.

2.   She was only interested in speaking to her target audience about her area expertise which is fine if you're a well -known speaker with brand recognition but new speakers generally have to expand their range and learn to speak on a variety of topics, including but not limited to business, women's subjects, etc. This increases her chances of getting booked for other gigs including her expert matter.

3.   When you're a new speaker trying to build a business with a limited budget, you have to adjust your way of thinking in terms of booking speaking gigs.

Barbara's philosophy was that she wanted to get speaking gigs without worrying about the business end of it like making money. For her, speaking was a way of getting her message out. As a speaker it should always have been about making money as well as getting her message out. Now to be clear I'm not saying that new speakers need to take every speaking gig that comes their way, however it doesn't hurt to be smart about which ones to take and how it will help build your over-all brand. To be honest if you're a struggling speaker (who is still building a brand) looking for an audience, can you really afford to turn down speaking opportunities that could lead to other speaking opportunities? Let me give you 2 examples. If you're a Jeffrey Hayzlett with a name brand and a following then you're probably not going to deviate from your list of topics. You may expand them but you're not going to damage the brand by deviating from the script. My second example comes from developing my own speaking repertoire. When I first began speaking over 30 years ago the only topic I spoke on was B2B telemarketing which worked for quite a number of years. And then around 2000 I began seeing a real decline in the number of sales professionals coming to my telemarketing workshops. It never occurred to me that I needed to expand my range until one attendee asked a sales question; which in retrospect made sense because you can't really talk about B2B telemarketing without talking about the next stage of closing a deal which is the sale. So developing a new sales workshop became the natural progression to the telemarketing talk. Surprisingly enough, once I thought about it, I actually had quite a bit to say on the subject. My next wake-up call came in the form of you guessed it, a workshop attendee asking if I had any tips on networking. This progressed into workshops on making money as a speaker, making money as a writer, launching a successful Internet radio show, launching a successful Internet magazine and making money in any economy which was the basis for my 3rd book. In fact this book came out of a number of speakers asking for tips on booking more engagements which turned into a successful workshop series and a booming booking service for speakers and authors. The moral of the story is that you can take a hard line in terms of speaking gigs and topics when you're well known, but not when you're trying to get people to know you and your work.

Being a struggling speaker means that you're primary goal is to get paid to share your wisdom. This also means that any speaking opportunity that comes your way should be treated like gold. I recently had 3 speaking opportunities figuratively fall in my lap. All came to me in an unusual fashion because I never thought any were my target audience. The first was via NAWBO (National Association of Women Business Owners) which was a 20 minute talk on how to make money by promoting yourself. This led to a second engagement at a larger NAWBO event (around 200 women) where I could make an offer and sell books etc., dinner included. The topic? Networking. Apparently the president of NAWBO (who was in the audience) was so impressed with my talk at the smaller event ,that she asked me to talk at the much larger venue. Two different talks. Two different gigs and multiple prospecting opportunities. The other gig came in the form of a speaking opportunity after my appearance on the Tonya Hofmann Show. Tonya, who is also the founder of Public Speakers Association, was so pleased with what I had to say that she immediately booked me to speak at her conference the following year. The third opportunity came from Compliance Unlimited which books and pays speakers to talk on a variety of subjects, mostly dealing with compliance issues. Since I had already given a webinar a few months prior they asked if I could speak on marketing and sales. What intrigued me was the fact that this company pays $1000 per day plus expenses (hard to say no to that). Long story short they have booked me to give several 2 day talks over the next year at $1000 a day.

Being in front of your target audience without actually trying to sell them something is also inconceivable. I'm not saying that your talk should sound like an infomercial but you should at least be prepared to make an offer to your audience, particularly if you're not getting paid to speak. Attendees want to know what other products and services you have to offer and if it's worth it for them to buy. How will they know if you're not willing to tell them? For me, the trick is to let attendees know about my services without actually giving them a hard sell. Instead I focus on offering great content that both gets their attention and persuades them to do business with me. In other words if the content is good enough then he must know what he's talking about. If he knows what he's talking about perhaps he's the right person to help me take my business to the next level. Or in simpler terms; is this person's info worth paying for?

Riding the waves

So awhile back I worked with a speaker who is extremely successful promoting herself as a six figure speaker(Very professional).Very personable and selective in terms of the prospects she takes on as clients; which at six figures annually she can afford to be. Her market and topic is also very selective which harkens back to a statement I make a lot. When you're generating six figures annually then you can speak on one topic without worry, but not when you're trying to get there, which is why new speakers always need to have more than one topic in their arsenal and why they struggle to book gigs. Here's what most speakers who complain about speaking for free don't realize. This speaker has figured out how to speak for free while making money by offering a great "ask". The "ask" in "speaker talk" is when the speaker asks the attendees to invest in their business future by purchasing something. This is perfectly acceptable because if a speaker is spending 90 minutes sharing their wisdom (for free) then they have every right to make an offer or sell a product. It's how we make our living after all. Now this particular speaker has figured out how to turn more than 20% of her attendees into paying customers by speaking for free. Plus what I've figured out (much to my surprise) is that even seasoned speakers have trouble converting "free" talks into sales which is why many speakers only last a short while in the business. See, this brilliant speaker has figured out that "the ask "is how the speaker will make money; on the back end. Truthfully? This tactic will not work for most speakers who are not at this skill level; because when you're generating six figures annually you're not really worried about making the rent per se.

What type of speaker are you?

Typically there are several types of speakers and multiple ways of getting paid to speak. I bring this up because as a speaker who also coaches, I noticed that many of my students who were new to the industry had no idea what type of speaker they wanted to be. Again this is important because what one charges as a coach is different from what a speaker might charge for a keynote. So here's a brief explanation along with a loose overview of what each might charge (again these are not hard and fast rules but rather a guide). The types of speakers include...

1. **The Coach-** This is the speaker who works primarily (but not exclusively) with individuals as well as groups. The coach is the speaker who might work with someone in a "bootcamp" setting, sharing all of the wisdom they've learned over the years. A coaching session may last one hour a week for several weeks or for just 1 hour. Typically coaches charge an hourly rate (I recommend a minimum of $175 to start and increasing based on experience). It's important to note that most speakers are also coaches.

2. **The Keynote-** A keynote speaker is someone who gives a speech (this should not be confused with a coach) to a room full of people for a flat fee (think Tony Robbins or Oprah). Most people who go into the speaking industry assume that they will be making "Keynote money" which can range from $2500+ for a 40 minute talk. Your rate should coincide with your expertise. For example, someone new to the industry wouldn't charge $100,000 for a speech because they don't have the experience to warrant that amount.

3. **The Seminar-**Again, this is where most speakers make their money and to be honest every speaker starts out by teaching a webinar, tele-seminar or a seminar. The speaker charges a nominal fee of say $49.00 per person for a 90 minute talk or can charge nothing instead

choosing to make money on the back end by making an offer or selling products services after the talk.

4. **The Triple Threat-** This is the speaker who does everything listed above but they may also have a preference. For example I can do all 3 but typically prefer to teach a seminar or act as a coach.

Diva at the podium

There is another type of speaker that isn't listed but should be noted just the same. This speaker for lack of a better name is "The Diva". These are the speakers that generally make their money from coaching individuals or groups but aren't quite as adept at booking gigs or closing deals. They typically will speak for the pleasure of having an audience and make their money by coaching. In fact most are terrific speakers but aren't great at the day to day running of their businesses (in my opinion). They forget appointments, lose files and will only speak under specific conditions (i.e. won't travel out of the area, or speak on any other topic other than their specific area of expertise) which is fine once you've built your business, and brand, but career suicide (in my opinion) for anyone trying to get to 6 figures. They aren't bad speakers; they would rather focus only on the speaking portion of their speaking business. And it *is* a business. What's ironic is that these speakers don't make much money speaking but feel the need to limit themselves on speaking opportunities (even paid ones) because the topic isn't something they're interested in or because they don't feel "experienced enough" to speak on an unfamiliar topic like say, project management and don't want to come across as a" phony". All of which I can respect even though I don't agree. Here's the thing. If someone is willing to pay you say $1000 a day plus expenses to speak on something as mundane as project management (and you're struggling to build your speaker business) then I say do your homework, come up with a talk to impress and take the money. I've had this conversation with a number of experienced speakers, most of whom have said the same thing, which is not to compromise who you are but be open to any and all speaking opportunities when you're trying to build your practice. One speaker that I tried in vain to coach, didn't listen to me and was very clear about what they wanted to do; which as it turned out was to speak on one subject and one subject only.

The problem was that this speaker's topic resonates only with a specific audience; meaning that if they're going to speak on say clinical depression and anxiety then they should be speaking at hospitals and clinics and associations that specialize in these topics. All of which are doable but take months to book because it's such a specialized industry as opposed to speaking in front of business groups which take less time to book and gives most speakers an audience capable of paying them for their work in less time. See the difference? To be clear, my advice to the speaker wasn't to give up speaking on her area of expertise but rather to expand her range of topics making her more marketable. This increases her opportunities for booking additional speaking gigs but her revenue as well.

The lesson is simple. Speaker one (the one mentioned earlier making six figures) has already developed a market that works and generates lots of revenue. They understand that in order to remain relevant they must always evolve their message and topics or risk being irrelevant to the audience. Speaker one is generating revenue and running their practice as a business. Is speaker one more selective in the selection of speaking opportunities? You bet. But speaker one is bringing in six figures a year and can afford to be picky. Speaker two has the right idea about staying true to the vision but goes about it in a way that will take her longer to reach that goal. Being unorganized, undisciplined and inflexible is a great way to limit your speaking engagements in major way.

Gia under pressure and building influence

I love referrals. And I love referring business to others .The reason I bring this up because one of the best ways to build a speaking practice is to get referred by someone else. There's' nothing like referring business to someone you know will appreciate it. I'm very lucky to have developed a network of influential people (but more on that later);but every once in a while you'll get a bad seed. These are the referrals that start off on the wrong foot and get progressively worse as time goes on. For example, one of my best clients referred me to an acquaintance who was looking for more speaking gigs. She and I had exchanged e-mails multiple times before speaking because she was far too busy to actually have a conversation with me. When we did finally connect, we agreed to a day and time (15 minutes) and a topic of discussion. After months of back and forth we were set to speak and on the day of the talk….

A.   She had no idea who I was or why I was calling

B.   Was outwardly hostile toward me because she was "on a deadline and really didn't have time to speak with me."

C.   She actually told me that she was "doing me a favor "by speaking with me.

D.   She only became interested in speaking with me after she learned about my successful radio show and" wouldn't she be a great guest"?

So not only was I not interested in doing business with this woman, but I had to ask myself if I would refer her. When my client contacted me and asked how the meeting went I tried to put the best spin on it as possible telling her that the meeting didn't go well but that it was possible that I had caught her on a bad day. When my client pressed me for more details, I had to level with her and tell her what actually happen which did not please her. Suffice it to say my client was not happy and has since cut ties with her. The bottom line is that the speaker community is a small one, the impression you put out could make the difference in booking more engagements or not.

King and Queen of America

Two of my best experiences working with speakers come from working with Beth and Bob. Beth is the more experienced of the two having spoken at corporations and women's groups. Both hired e to book engagements but for different reasons. Beth having more public speaking gigs under her belt wanted more exposure as well as diversity in her speaking; while Bob needed more help with business development as well as bookings in the media not to mention speaking gigs. What's great about working with these two dynamic individuals is that despite their experience, both sought out my help and advice. In my opinion, there's nothing wrong with asking for help when you need it; particularly if you're willing to listen to the advice given.

When an event goes wrong: Top 10 tips to salvage a bad event

It happens to everyone. Despite all of the planning, marketing, and promotion your event falls short. So here are my top tips to hedge your bets for a more successful event the next time around......

1.   Don't panic, get angry or stressed out(during the talk). It just makes you look unprofessional and like a spoiled brat in front of your peers. It also keeps you from thinking things thru to find a solution. There will be plenty of time after the event to really lose it. What's important to remember is...

A.   If it doesn't turn out well, it isn't the end of the world. Learn and move on

B.   This is a small (if embarrassing) hiccup in the bigger scheme of things. Think of everything one goes thru in life and business especially the bad things. Think of every lousy thing you've ever endured including divorce, bankruptcy, homelessness, illness. If low attendance at an event is the worst thing to ever happen to you, then you're doing pretty well and probably won't die of embarrassment.

2.   Give yourself a maximum of 3 days to feel bad after the event. Learn from it and then get on with it. You are allowed to feel like crap because of a low turnout but you are NOT allowed to stay in mourning over one bad event longer than a few days. You've got more important things to do so grieve for a minute and then get on with it.

3.   Make a checklist during the planning process to ensure that you haven't forgotten anything.

4.   Confirm everything up to a week before the event. Things happen and can go wrong in a heartbeat. Vendors can flake and as lame as it sounds, people forget; even when you're paying them. So make sure to confirm everything to save yourself some drama.

5.   Document everything via e-mail, particularly if you're working with a team. Do not leave it up to chance or a verbal agreement.

6.   Set deadlines so that everyone involved in the planning knows and understands the time table.

7.　　Plan up to 3 months in advance. This sounds like a long lead time for planning an event but trust me, at stress o'clock, you'll be glad for the breathing room.

8.　　Partner with others that can help you promote your event. Even better, partner with a well-known brand to help get the word out. For example, I've partnered with the GGBA (Golden Gate Business Association) and the Payne Mansion to cross promote the event because it benefits everyone involved.

9.　　When putting together your event, make sure to choose people that can actually help you with your event. Over the years I've chosen to work with people that promised to help but when crunch time approached, couldn't be found. The excuses varied but really boiled down to being "too busy". So now I try and choose more carefully, partnering with people that can not only help plan the event but can execute and (really important) show up for the event. My philosophy has always been to try and show up for as many events (of my friends and supporters) as possible. The theory is that you can't expect others to support you if you don't support them.

10.　　Have a plan B and C. when things go wrong. And things always go wrong. The trick is to have a backup just in case. I find that having a backup takes the stress out of planning.

Chapter Three: Planning your first talk

So you've decided to finally host your first professional talk. Here are some tips to make teaching your first workshop or seminar a success.

1.　　Decide on a date-Always give yourself a few months to plan and promote your workshop

2.　　Decide on a venue – Including Intellegentoffice.com, Davinci.com, Fort Mason Center or any place that has meeting/conference rooms. Most have special discounts on a regular basis. Booking at least 3 months in advance is advisable.

3.　　Next figure out your subject matter-What subject matter can you teach that has mass appeal? Be sure to write down some key bullet points to stay on track during the workshop.

4.　　Decide how much to charge-Some speaking engagements will be pro bono. For example if you're a member of the Chamber you can give a short lecture on your subject matter to a room full of prospects however you won't make any immediate money. The real money comes from making an offer after the talk. However you can also host a small workshop and charge as little as $49 per person. Be sure to charge enough to cover your costs and show a profit.

5.   Be sure to contact industry specific organizations about getting booked as a guest speaker- It's as simple as deciding which organizations you'd like to work with ,contacting the person in charge of bookings and asking if they will be booking speakers at future events. Be sure to Google to find associations in your area.

6.   Contact your local Small Business Development Center/Small Business Administration/Library about consulting or teaching classes. SBA doesn't pay speakers however SBDC and the library will generally have a budget allocated for speakers. A relatively new function of your local library comes in the form of Small Business Workshops. Be sure to ask for the person booking the business workshops for the library. Here's the great news. Most have a budget to pay their instructors and pay can range from $25-150.00 per hour.

7.   Okay, I've mentioned the SBA a few times and it's still worth repeating. While the Small Business Administration will not pay you for your services it is still an excellent way to get your firm's name in front of a targeted audience and increase your database. Once you've gathered contact information be sure to follow up with a thank you e-mail and basic info on your services. Follow up that e-mail with a phone call to make sure they've received and read the e-mail. Some e-mails are never read because they wind up in spam. I must caution you however. While the SBA encourages the private sector to create workshops to educate new business owners, they cannot endorse any one company and frown on self-promotion.

8.   Contact the Learning Annex-They will promote your event, book the room and pay you a percentage of the money made from attendance. All you have to do is show up.

9.   Use sites like Eventbrite to promote your event which helps your cash flow if you accept payments via PayPal.

10.   Post on free event websites to make sure you get the word out about your event to your audience.

11.   Teach at schools like CIIS, Academy of Art and other schools by tailoring your subject matter to fit your audience.

13.   Think globally. Contact prospects outside of your geographical area. This is a great option particularly if you're going for more of a global audience (webinar) rather than a local one. This tip has become more and more important to my company's well-being over the last few years. As small business owners we're not taught to think in terms of international or multi-geographical sales. Often we're aware of the potential only after we figure out that people outside of our city or state are willing to pay for our services (an epiphany that came to me many years ago). This became even more apparent several years ago when the economy was still in the toilet and very few firms in California (where I live) were making money (many went out of business) which is why tele-seminars work so well for my firm. Lots of profits with none of the overhead. It also allows me the chance to market my services globally and expand my market.

14.   Offer services such as consulting, at a discount or reduced rate to close even more sales at events. Everyone loves a good deal and so what you're looking to do is create an easy "yes" for workshop attendees.

15 .Launch your own internet radio show. This is an unconventional tips; and there's a caveat to this. First only launch a show if you actually have something interesting to say. In fact, if you have many things to say it's even better. No one wants to listen to a show with a lot of dead air. Next, offer a show that's of interest and service to others. The concept for my show Small Business Forum www.blogtalkradio.com/tonywilkins started out as a short 30 minute radio show offering marketing and sales tips from industry experts. Somewhere along the way the format changed to a show for and about small business where I invite small business experts on to discuss their work and offer useful tips to my listeners. The show became an overnight success sparking a new 1 hour format with advertisers and a six month waiting list.

A. It gets you exposure. An internet show is a great way to expand your clientele base globally while promoting your work. The rules for broadcasting on the internet are different than traditional radio because you won't have the FCC breathing down your neck. You can make your show as long or short as you like and on virtually any subject.

B. It allows you to expand your brand to a global audience.

c. It helps you develop new skills (like media interviews) which you can use to springboard into other professional areas (TV anyone?)

D. One benefit to hosting a show is the level of attention you garner from your peers. This became apparent when most of the attendees of a recent networking event knew who I was (and wanted to meet me) before I had even introduced myself to anyone. I think it was the first time in my career where I ever felt validated in my work.

The 5 things to know before booking your first talk

1.   Charge enough to cover expenses

2.   Make the cost affordable to attendees

3.   Promote as much as possible

4.   Show up even if it's just 1 person since that $49 attendee could turn into a $300 an hour client for the next year.

5.   Promote books and any other services at the event

6.   Never provide handouts. Handouts (in my opinion) make attendees apathetic in terms of actually paying attention to the information being taught in the class. To me it's like giving the answers to a test to your students. If they already have your notes then there's no reason to contact you further.

This is especially important if your goal is to sell products and services after the talk. Essentially what you're doing (by not providing handouts) is laying the groundwork for attendees to contact you for info, resources etc.

7.   Collect business cards from attendees to sell services after the event

Tips from a professional booker

So a few years ago I launched a booking service for speakers. I figured that because I was always on the lookout for speaking opportunities and most of my acquaintances in the speaking community were too, this would be a great way to marry the two ideas into a new money making venture. I assumed that I would get a few clients here and there, just enough to keep me busy but not enough to inhibit me from advancing my own speaking career. Little did I know as the saying goes…. Fast forward to the present and my service currently books more than 15 speakers into paid, non- paid and media opportunities on a monthly basis. The reason that the service is so successful is because I realized that there was a need given that nearly every speaker I interviewed for my show asked the same question. Where are the speaking gigs and how do I book more of them? Some of the speakers I work with are relatively new to the game (while others have been at it for some time and just need to fill their calendar) and so you won't find me working with someone that books more than say 20 speaking gigs per month. These are the speakers that need and want the exposure as well as the opportunity to get their message out. So in addition to booking them I also coach them on how to get more gigs. Most will listen to any advice I give them and those that don't are usually rotated out of the system. My theory is that I can help anyone that takes an active part in their success but I can't take part (or be blamed) for their failure. If speakers are gaining more speaking opportunities with me than without me then I feel that I've done my job. So with that in mind I've compiled a list of my top tips for speakers from someone that books speakers on a regular basis.

Top 5

1.   Have a one sheet that sells you. Part of my job isn't to sell the decision maker on the speaker. My job is to send a one sheet that gets the attention of the planner, follow up with an e-mail and phone call and determine what type of speaker the event planner is looking for while attempting to book the speaker for that venue. I don't negotiate rates or travel amenities (leaving that to the speaker to handle). So essentially my job is to get the speaker's foot in the door and book where appropriate. The problem with most one sheets is that while many are good enough to impress the event planner if the event planner is looking for a general type of speaker (i.e. motivational) it can be a bit too focused to get the speaker a gig if the event planner is looking to book for more of a variety of speakers. For example, if your speaker sheet only lists you as a motivational speaker (ignoring the fact that you're also a business/sales/ marketing expert) the event planner will assume that you're only interested in booking motivational talks. Which is fine if that's all you want to do and have built an impressive speaking resume and aren't hurting for gigs or money. However for most speakers who want the audience and the revenue, having a more diverse one sheet is probably going to serve you better by opening more opportunities to you. So the bottom line is that it's perfectly fine to have a specialty if you're making 6 figures but not if you're just starting out.

2.   Don't blow off *any* speaking opportunity. One of the biggest killers to a speaking career is failing to show up for a booked gig. Don't laugh; it happens more often than you know and is one of my biggest pet peeves because most gigs take weeks sometimes months to book. I currently work with a speaker, perfectly lovely woman who was booked for one of the largest speaking opportunities in the Bay Area-Small Business Week. This is a week of networking, workshops and promotion of small business. The

event planner who is in charge of booking speakers spend months figuring out which speakers and topics they want to cover for each event. To say that they are very selective is an understatement because bookers like myself, work diligently to get their clients in to speak. Why is this a hot ticket? First you should understand that a lot of planning goes into putting each event together, the planners also handle the marketing and book attendees (usually about 100) into each workshop. After much promotion of both the speaker and the workshop they compile a list of attendees into an Excel spread sheet which is then sent to each speaker. That alone makes this a major reason for speakers to show up. (As a matter of fact 4 of my speakers including myself were chosen to speak which took weeks to set up). So when a speaker forgets to show up and the event planner is left scrambling to find a replacement, it reflects badly on them and me. How did I handle it? First I got on the phone to the speaker to find out if he was dead or in the hospital or if he needed me to send someone to help him get there. The speaker was absolutely mortified which is why I didn't drop her as a client right then and there. She explained that she had confused her speaking gig the previous day at the SBA(a much smaller venue) with SBW(a much larger gig). The second thing I suggested was that she contact the planner immediately and apologize profusely for the screw up. The third thing I did was give them a lecture on never making that mistake in the future. Now many of you would say that a lecture was unnecessary but I disagree. Here's the thing, if I've worked tirelessly for weeks to get you an A+ speaking gig and you don't show up and don't call, thereby damaging my rep with the event planner who I deal with annually then you're entitled to a lecture. Not enough to belittle you but just enough so that you never make that mistake again on my watch.

3.   Hiring a telemarketer for $10 an hour to make calls just for you isn't the same as hiring a booker to rep you. I had another client that complained that she wasn't getting enough bookings and wondered aloud to me whether or not it might be more prudent for her to hire someone for $10 an hour to do what I do. Now it's important to note that this speaker was paying less than all of my other speakers because she was a referral and I wanted the business. However she was also a speaker with a niche market making it difficult to book her in her target market not to mention any business organization like NAWBO. As always, I suggest expanding her market to discuss topics appropriate to women and business owners and especially running a business. Naturally she said no. I managed to book her into some speaking engagements that were appropriate for her market and she complained that no one bought from her deeming the experience a failure. I also suggested that she pepper any speaking engagement with people that she wanted to do business with which would increase her chances at closing a sale. She never did this, complaining that she was too busy and had too much on her plate. So after she queried if hiring a $10 an hour telemarketer might be a better fit for her, I suggested that she do just that. I've never looked back. See here's the thing. You have to do whatever is best for your business and if that means hiring someone for less money to do something as taxing as spending weeks or months trying to book a speaker into a venue then I say have at it and all the best. What a booker does is just about everything a speaker might do for themselves short of actually closing the deal. If someone will do the same job long term for $10 an hour than more power to them because I'm not that guy. The bottom line is that you get what you pay for.

4.   Book in your market as well as business groups. So the client I spoke of earlier has a very specific niche and not interested in booking talks at the local NAWBO Chapter which I feel is a mistake. First, whatever your market you should always ensure that you're in front of an audience that can actually afford to pay for your services after your talk. So while speaking to your niche market is a good idea it can also take more time to book. Why? Let's say that you speak on anxiety and stress and would like to speak at the Asperger's Association (which is what this client requested). Sounds reasonable right? Of course except for a few issues.

A.   The Asperger Association might not be looking for speakers at that time and may only book speakers on an as needed basis or may have already booked their quota for the year.

B.   Opening your market to other opportunities in the business community will ensure that your audience is able to afford your services after your talk. It also means that you'll be booked for more speaking opportunities sooner because business groups are always looking for speakers and book them weeks, sometimes months in advance. So it's really about timing and getting on their radar at the right time. The more you can tailor your talk to a bankable audience, the more speaking opportunities you're likely to book.

5.   Read your e-mail and mark your calendar. Another one of my pet peeves is a speaker that complains about the lack of speaking gigs while missing opportunities that are right in front of them. I can't tell you how many times I will send a weekly update to a speaker mentioning in my e-mail to be sure to look at a specific file because it contains a speaking opportunity or has a deadline for submitting a proposal for a gig (I don't submit proposals because with 15 clients it would take me forever if I submit a proposal for each one). I can't tell you the number of times a client will find e-mail weeks after an event and say "I never saw this or when did you send this". Obviously the e-mail had been sent weeks (or even months) prior but because the speaker was too busy or had too much on their plate, the inevitable speaking opportunity slips past them. I get it and it happens but losing a speaking gig because you were too busy is like throwing money out the window while wondering where your wallet went.

6.   Work the leads from all of your speaking engagements. We're all six degrees of separation from someone that can help us get our next gig. What's surprising are the number of speakers that speak in front of a packed house but never follow up with any of the attendees after the event(it happens). Many sales don't happen at the event. Usually it takes a few weeks for planners to read over all of your material and then decide based on the great talk you gave to hire you. And with all things sales oriented there must be….

A.   A need for the product or service.

B.   A budget or the ability to be able to afford the product or service.

C.   And the prospect must be open to doing business

D.   And the sale must be a priority. In other words, the prospect needs the service or product within 1-3 months or a reasonable period of time.

E.   If there is no need, budget, or if it isn't a priority, then there is no sale and in many cases there isn't even a booking to speak.

7.   Whenever you start a new marketing campaign, work the leads that are already in your database- first. Coming from a business development background one of the first things you learn is not to overlook the leads already in your database. If you've been speaking for any amount of time, chances are you've accumulated a number of prospects that have either A) Booked you to speak. B) Weren't interested in booking you at this time. C) Requested information or a one sheet be sent to them. D) Asked that you to follow up in 1,3,6 months or so when they will be looking for speakers. It's also probable that unless you've got a really great system for managing leads you've forgotten all about these leads. So the real question is what's happened to these leads and is anyone following up on them and if so, how often? The number one reason for lack of sales is lack of follow up. Think of everyone that you've made contact with and spoken in front of. Have you asked them about upcoming events that need speakers? Have you kept track of these leads? How are you keeping track?

8.   Pick up the phone yourself. Okay now many of you are going to disagree with this but the truth is that if you want more speaking gigs, you're going to have to pick up the phone yourself. That isn't to say that you can't hire someone to follow up on leads for you. What I'm saying is that we all have contacts that we've developed over the years that perhaps require a more personal touch. No one can market you better than you. No one can tell your story better than you; or tell an event planner why you need to be on the schedule for their next event. Even if that isn't the case, are you really so busy with speaking dates that you can't be bothered to make a phone call?

9.   Wow the audience and deliver a thought provoking talk. Many speakers give good talks. Some even deliver great talks. But how many deliver thought provoking talks. These are the talks that leave the audience with a new way of thinking about things regardless of the subject. And the speakers that deliver these talks are the ones that get booked time and again for future talks. Remember the way to determine if you've given a great talk is if it leads to another booking or more business.

Chapter Four: What kind of speaker are you?

Don't limit your talk. How some speakers are doing themselves a disservice by limiting their topics

I love my clients. There is nothing better than working with customers that get it. But occasionally I'll land a customer that won't listen to any of my advice in terms of booking more engagements. These are the speakers that speak on one subject only. Professionally, "there's nothing wrong with choosing a topic and sticking to it "states speaker and talk show host Jeffrey Hayzlett. Jeff is an in demand speaker and author of the best-selling "Think big, Act bigger "as well as a frequent guest on MSNBC and The Apprentice (he calls Donald Trump friend). Jeff is considered a "top tiered" speaker commanding thousands of dollars for speaking engagements. Jeff and I agree on this point but with a slight addendum. Jeffrey has years of experience under his belt which means that he's built a brand and doesn't deviate from it. However, when you're not as well-known what should a speaker do to land gigs?

Here's the thing about booking gigs; they take time to develop (even the pro bono gigs). And if you're one sheet reads as if you'll appeal to a limited audience then you'll be sorely disappointed by the response you'll generate from planners. Here are a couple of examples...

One client very early in my booking career was initially interested in whatever bookings I could land her regardless of location. She could do this because a family member (working for one of the big airlines) could fly her anywhere in the U.S. for free (she only had to pay for accommodations). It's important to note that this speaker had written many books on a variety of topics but for the most part humorous anecdotes, short stories and fiction. Since she was also a business person I felt that it only made sense to book her for more business related events since booking an author for literary conferences can be a bit more challenging. This way she could capitalize on her brand as a business owner as well as an author. So I booked this speaker for a number of speaking engagements at various SBA (not her market and she couldn't sell books). I tried booking her at NAWBO (National Association of Women Business Owners) SBA and several business and literary organizations; but to no avail. I was able to book some speaking engagements for her but most planners just weren't interested. The problem (which I cautioned her about repeatedly) lay in her one sheet which read like a letter to a buddy instead of a list of business accomplishments. A one sheet is like a resume for speakers. If you're trying to get booked to speak it should reflect topics that will most likely be of interest to planners. Sending a one sheet about "learning to laugh out loud through controversy" isn't enough to get the attention of any planner. It's up to the speaker to give a planner a reason to book them particularly if they are speaking to a business audience (i.e. people who can afford to pay you after you speak). The moral of the story is that I never made the mistake of booking another speaker who can't tailor their talk to their audience.

Chapter Five: Creating a marketing platform that fills seats

Investing in your business 101: Spending money on marketing and advertising: What you need to know before you write the check....

I recently had a conversation with a client who was complaining that none of his marketing and advertising efforts were paying off and wondered what he could do to turn things around. So instead of giving a pat answer I decided to write down and send him some of my best tips for getting the most out of a new marketing and/or advertising campaign. I hope you find them helpful.

1.   Advertising and marketing are <u>not</u> the same thing. Advertising is about selling your product or service whereas marketing is about promoting the product to your target audience. Both can be effective if done correctly and over a period of time and if you know what you want to achieve with each. Why are you advertising? What do you want to get from your marketing campaign?

2.   Buying advertising doesn't guarantee sales. For example, if you're planning on spending ad dollars as the owner of a small business owner, ask yourself the following….

A.   Who is your target audience?

B.   What's your monthly budget?

C.   What are you expecting from your campaign?

D.   Most owners of small businesses spend dollars on marketing but not advertising. So the real question is what are your expectations from each and how will you measure its success?

E.   How often will you run your campaign?

F.   There are many forms of advertising and marketing. Which form will you use? Here's a sample: Marketing: Telemarketing, e-mail, direct mail.

Advertising: Print, pay per click, digital

3. A decent e-mail or direct mail campaign can cost little or no money to produce but is best when utilizing a platform like Constant Contact or Vistaprint.com. On the other hand, a good telemarketing campaign can cost thousands but generate a faster ROI(Let's not forget that after sending a direct mail or e-mail piece, you must still follow up with a phone call). The trick with any marketing or ad campaign is targeting your audience and consistently keeping your name in front of them over long periods of time.

4. E-mail- A good marketing campaign-relies on consistently marketing your product over long periods of time. Where things go awry is when it's marketed to the wrong audience or when it's performed over too short a period of time. The message must also be clear with a call to action (call now to take advantage of this offer) and offer a reason to contact the business owner. Another reason a campaign might not work is lack of follow up.

5.Follow up is key-If you're going to spend the time and money that it takes to send a great marketing piece out, wouldn't you also want to make sure it reached your intended audience not to mention learn what they thought of the piece? In order to follow up properly you need a fool proof telemarketing plan.

6.Telemarketing-If you're new to utilizing a telemarketing campaign here's the secret. There are several tricks to setting up an effective campaign. First start small with 1-2 tms instead of a full boiler room of cold callers. This gives you the opportunity to test the campaign, find out what works and what doesn't. After you've generated some consistency you can expand and add to your team. Typically this is accomplished with a decent appointment/sales campaign. If hiring someone isn't in the budget I would recommend doing the calling yourself (at first). Even if you can afford to hire a team, it's important to test the program yourself by making some calls yourself. Nothing will make you appreciate a good telemarketer more than understanding what they have to go thru to get an appointment/sale for you. I recommend at least 2 months of calling (16 hrs a week by the business owner) to really get a feel for what works and doesn't. Unfortunately most business owners can't be bothered; which is why there's no follow up and lack of sales.

If/when you hire someone, be sure to pay them a decent wage; somewhere in the neighborhood of $20 an hour if no commission. This may be expensive but consider the fact that the person doing the calling is trying to help you build your business. How long can you expect to keep any professional interested in working for you if you're only paying them $10 an hour?

Help!! I want to set up a cold calling team but don't know how to get started....

So as many of you know I began my career as a B2B telemarketer, setting appointments for insurance agents, mortgage brokers and everyone in between. I was so proficient in my work that at one point I was the highest paid telemarketer in Chicago. Expanding my practice, I became a much sought after consultant and coach a writer for several websites and finally the author of the best-selling, Telemarketing Success for Small and Mid -Size Firms. I've set up telemarketing departments and managed and trained thousands of professionals over a 30 year career. But all things eventually come to an end and so (a few years ago) I decided that it was time to focus on my speaking career and leave the telemarketing consulting behind (a smart decision considering that I'm, making more money and have never been happier). I haven't really given too much thought about my past career as a telemarketer until I received a call from someone who was a regular reader of my column on Examiner.com (not that regular since I haven't written for the site for several years; but I won't quibble). The reader/fan contacted me and asked if I would call him to advise him on setting up a telemarketing department, which I was happy to oblige. After a 45 minute conversation and an agreement to send info on my workshops (again he wasn't aware of the fact that I hadn't been in telemarketing for several years) I came to several realizations that I'd like to share, just in case you'd like to set up a team of your own.

1.   Decide on a budget before doing anything. As with anything, your budget will determine whether you hire 1 telemarketer for 30 hours at $15 per hour for 3 months; or 2 telemarketers for 10 hours at $20 per hour for a month. It's all about your need and your wallet at this point. Know exactly what you want to pay and how often.

2.   Pay them what they're worth. What I find interesting is the fact that someone that makes over $200,000 a year will only pay a telemarketer (i.e. the person helping you close sales) a $5 per hour wage (which I found out is the going rate in the Philippines) and yet expect the telemarketer to speak perfect

English, stick around for more the 90 days and generate 20 appointments per week (trust me I've heard these numbers over the years). So my suggestion (regardless of where you live in the world and based on budget and experience) is to pay a telemarketer their worth meaning an hourly living wage of say $15-$20 per hour plus a nice commission. There are several reasons to do this. First, you never want the person responsible for helping to generate sales for your firm to have to worry about paying the rent. If they know they're receiving a weekly stipend then it allows them to focus on the task at hand. Second, most telemarketers are not business owners unless they're like me and actually own the firm. Asking a telemarketer to work on commission for someone else is like asking them to work for free until you sell something which (let's be honest) can take weeks if not months. By that time your telemarketer is now behind on rent and bouncing checks left and right. See it's not about offering a telemarketer a large commission if you sell something because by the time you do their financial situation is in free fall. Many telemarketers are independent contractors and thus already work for themselves. So if they're only getting paid if they close a deal for their own company, why would they work for someone else and expect to work on commission (regardless of the amount)?

3.   Start small and grow from there. As I mentioned earlier, I spent a great deal of time on the phone with this business owner who made no secret of his need to keep expenses down. So I advised him to keep his expenses down by hiring only one or two telemarketers at a time growing his team as needed.

4.   "I can't keep telemarketers for long". I hear this one a lot and here's where business owners miss the boat. You do get what you pay for". If someone only paid me minimum wage for my talent, how long would you expect me to stick around? It's fine to pay other people a small wage if you think it's going to get you what you want, however those of us that are actually writing the check would never accept a low wage because we couldn't live on it. And yet we expect others to not only do so but to be okay with it. Here's the thing, any telemarketer with more than 5 years of experience, and is worth keeping around for any decent amount of time should be paid what they're worth. So if you're thinking of paying them $5.00 an hour and expecting them to stick around, then you're kidding yourself. It's the reason most telemarketers get a rep for being flaky. It's not that we have short attention spans, it's just that we're not sticking around for less than what we know we're worth; particularly if we don't see a sign for advancement.

5.   Telemarketers are part of your team. One mistake people make when hiring a telemarketer is the fact that they don't see us as part of their sales team but more like disposable labor. It's part of the reason we don't stick around any one job for very long. We know that we're not valued and so we're off to the next better paying gig as soon as possible. We are the last to get paid (if at all) and the first to get cut when business is slow. And so our first inclination is to take care of ourselves first.

6.   Hiring someone to read a script isn't the same as hiring someone to think. It's fine if you just want to hire someone to make calls and read scripts however, the difference between hiring a script reader and someone that can think when talking to prospects, is miles apart. The difference is that a script reader, reads scripts and a thinker doesn't need a script to get the job done because they already know how to hold a conversation.

7.   Don't burn them out. A telemarketer is a human being and not a robo caller. Many business owners hire telemarketers thinking that they should be able to make hundreds of phone calls per hour without stopping. And then these same business owners wonder why...

A.   The telemarketer is burnt out after only a few months on the job.

B.   Is turning in sloppy work or leads/appointments that aren't valid

C.   Appears to be lethargic.

Telemarketing is like long distance running. If you burn out in the first mile then you'll never make it to the finish line.

8.   Be clear in your expectations and goals. When I was telemarketing full time I would begin every relationship by first having a conversation via telephone. After which I would begin having a dialogue via e-mails (always have info in written form in case you need to revert back to a conversation). One of the problems with working with a telemarketer is that there is a disconnect between what the business owners wants and what the telemarketer can do.

9.   Communicate on a regular basis. While I don't like incessant e-mails from clients I do like at least a weekly e-mail from them letting me know that they received updates etc.

10.   No employees like to be micromanaged. The fan that I had a phone conversation with was very concerned with how to manage the telemarketer. He was considering recording the conversations (which is illegal in most states without consent from both parties). Here's the thing. If you're hiring a professional, treat them as a professional. If you were hiring say a lawyer or an accountant who typically wouldn't be working in your office, then you wouldn't expect to have a camera or a recording to make sure they are billing you correctly. It's the same thing with any profession including telemarketers (and yes a good many of us are very professional and treat it as a career).

11.   Make calls yourself before hiring anyone. One of the best ways to find out if a telemarketing campaign will be successful is to make calls yourself. This will give you a good sense of what works and what doesn't. It will also give insight into what to expect from your next telemarketer.

Chapter Six: The difference between pro bono and paid gigs and why both are important

When Pro Bono is detrimental to your speaking career

I host a networking group the second Friday of every month. We have business professionals from around the country calling in looking for support, contacts, whatever. On a recent call, one of my members (a speaker) mentioned that she was mentoring numerous start -ups and women owned business owners including lecturing and consulting several times a month. Her problem unfortunately was that she wasn't generating as much revenue as she'd like. And while she was clearly frustrated, she wasn't really looking to change her M.O. until I asked her one question. When did you start a non-profit? Naturally the question left her speechless. Her mind hadn't allowed for the fact that she was now essentially giving her product away for free. But the kicker was that she didn't know when her business had become primarily pro bono. But this scenario happens more than you think.

New speakers or speakers trying to build a following are always looking for ways to get the word out about their work. That means any opportunity to speak is a good opportunity; money is secondary to some speakers because to them it's all about exposure. And so these speakers will take nearly any opportunity to have their messages heard by the right people even without getting paid. Here's my view. I tend to do a certain number of pro bono engagements per year. However, even before I agree to a pro bono gig, I try and make sure at least most of my criteria are met….

A.   Who is my audience? I tend to work with small business owners, sales professionals, and anyone looking to increase sales, productivity or clientele. So a room full of startups looking for money wouldn't be my target audience. If the group isn't likely to buy a book or hire me as a consultant, then I will more often than not turn the offer down.

B.   Are there amenities? If I'm not getting paid to speak but the decision maker is willing to cover expenses and the audience is my market; I might accept the opportunity.

C.   If they (the decision makers) are willing to partner with me on another event where their brand means ticket sales then I'm more likely to accept the opportunity. An example of this is partnering with a Wells Fargo or other large corporation where it makes sense to use their brand to get in front of my target audience.

D.   Again, your first option should always be a paying gig but when that's not possible, use the pro bono gig to your advantage. For example, I speak in front of a group of about 100 business owners once a year for small business week. It's always very well attended and the organizers always handle the marketing and promotion for the event (all I do is show up and teach). However I'm not allowed to promote my work during the lecture. My way around this rule is to exchange cards with attendees (the organizers also send the list of attendees to instructors as well). This increases my database exponentially, and truth be told if I can't close a few sales out of 100 attendees then I'm in the wrong business.

Making the switch –Weighing the options of accepting pro bono gigs also means redistributing the wealth a bit. That means approx. 85% of my speaking gigs should be paid while any pro bono work should allow access to the attendee list(if I can get both all the better). For new speakers, accepting even a small honorarium is a step closer to this number. And don't forget asking for testimonials and referrals will put you in a better position for getting more paid speaking gigs.

Let me be clear. I don't have a problem with pro bono speaking (mostly because I can usually convert them into money makers). Many speakers however, haven't figured out how to convert pro bono gigs into revenue, leaving them frustrated and essentially running a nonprofit. As I've mentioned a pro bono gig is only considered "speaking for free "if it doesn't result in the following...

   A. A second speaking opportunity. One reason speakers speak is to gain exposure. In order for a pro bono gig to be worth a speaker's time they have to get something out of it. So if a speaker has given an audience great content, one would hope that this would lead to additional speaking gigs (it's one reason I always recommend that speakers pepper the room with meeting planners who might book them for additional opportunities).
   B. A sale or sales. The ultimate goal for any speaking is to close sales and land clients. This is why many speakers sell from the stage, sell from the back of the room or sell after the event. If you're not generating sales from an audience of say 10 people then, yes you are speaking for free. As a booker of speakers I can get your foot in the door but it's up to you as the speaker to close the sale. Again whether you're speaking to a room of 1 or 100 your job is to give great content and close a sale. Period.
   C. Increase database and exposure. We all want exposure which is just one of the many reasons speakers speak for "free". But gaining exposure is only good if you can also obtain contact info

from attendees. For example, let's say that you've spoken in front of say 75 people but you never bothered to gain contact info from attendees(I've had speakers that have done this and then wonder why they aren't closing sales). You've gained exposure, which is great, but you have nothing else to show for it.

Remember. If you're doing anything other than what's listed, then you're working for free.

Chapter Seven: How much should I charge? And how to get paid.

"You know you're not charging enough when they sound relieved that it's so little and buy with no hesitation, it's time to test higher pricing! Ben Gay III Exec. Director for the Natl. Assoc. of Professional Salespeople

How much should I charge?

This is one of the more frequent questions I receive from speakers (along with wondering where all the speaking gigs are). And truth be told there are a few ways to make money from speaking which include (but not limited to)...

1.   Coaching- I made quite a bit of money as a coach, primarily working with small business owners and sales professionals helping them generate more revenue. Coaching is what most consultants do and is usually the foundation for everything else we do. If you're a coach/consultant then you're probably charging anywhere from $150+ per hour. My coaching spans many topics including sales training, telemarketing, networking essentially close to 30 different topics. Because I've got over 30 years' experience in business my hourly of $350 is commensurate with my experience. I also have a minimum number of hours (20) that I require each client to commit to when they sign with me.

2.   Mentoring- This has become more and more popular within the speaking community in recent years and is most effective when charging an hourly rate commiserate with your experience. Mentoring (in my opinion) is different from coaching because mentoring is about guiding the mentee and taking them under your wing; whereas coaching is about offering tips and suggestions and sharing your experience. It's a subtle difference but there is a difference.

3.   Keynote. Keynote speaking isn't for everyone and part of the reason I decided to explain the difference is because most new speakers don't understand the difference between keynote speaking and speaking as a coach or hosting a seminar. Keynote speakers like Tony Robbins charge a premium to address large audiences (thousands). When you're at that level you're not coaching per se unless it's on a large scale. It's more about selling dvd's and selling out stadiums (nothing wrong with that, by the way) than coaching which is what we as speakers aspire to. Keynote speaking is not for everyone since it takes a rare type of speaker to deliver a keynote dynamic speech. But those that do will undoubtable make a very good living at it.

4.   A couple of things to note. Most event planners will not take you seriously if you're not charging a minimum of $2500 per keynote speech (at the low end). Speakers like Tony Robbins and Jeff Hayzlett rack in millions by charging on the higher end which can range from $25,000+ per speech. So anyone that is in high demand can easily make 6-7 figures just as a keynote speaker. Here's the key though. In order to command that much you really have to be worth it. What decision makers hate to see is a $2500 speaker charging $25,000 for a speech. If you can't deliver a powerful and dynamic talk, then don't expect to be asked back for future engagements (not to mention all the prospects sitting in the audience). So the real question is this. What kind of speaker are you really?

5.   Hosting events-One way to make money as a speaker is by hosting an event. Hosting an event takes a special type of business professional and speaker. This isn't about hosting a networking event, what I'm talking about is hosting a conference or summit to give yourself and possibly other speakers an opportunity to speak in front of an audience. Most speakers actually hate hosting because it takes a lot of time and energy to pull off a successful conference. The amount of time and energy it takes to

produce an event can be overwhelming and can feel like a full time job at times but hang in there. Here are a few tips to keep in mind when hosting an event.

A.   Plan ahead. The more ambitious the event the more time you'll need. It's the promotion and the little details that take up so much time. Think about who you want in the audience. Are you inviting CEO'S and event planners? Entrepreneurs or industry specific professionals like insurance agents? Next decide on your topic. Does it fit with your target audience? What's your price compared to your overhead? Are you charging enough to show a profit after expenses?

B.   Keep planning. I like to give myself a minimum of 3 months to plan any event especially if it's a seminar and not a webinar. At this writing I have several conferences that I'm planning 6-9 months out mostly because there are multiple components to each event that need managing. And because each event is going to not only showcase my work but the work of all the speakers in attendance then I have to promote each event well in advance.

C.   Get others to pitch in and in some cases chip in. So after hosting many events (some more successful than others) I've learned to ask each speaker to be accountable for filling seats. What I've learned from past experience is that when you're the host of an event, some speakers typically will expect you to handle all of the heavy lifting including all of the promotion while they take center stage. And unless you've hosted a large scale event then most (not all) are oblivious to what goes into hosting a successful event. In fact most promoters will agree that many speakers aren't even aware when something goes wrong at an event because by the time they know anything (if ever) it's been handled. One of my rules for hosting events that feature other speakers is to make each speaker accountable for filling a minimum number of seats (usually around 10 per speaker). I made this decision based on the fact that in the past many speakers would ask to speak at one of my events but did nothing to promote it to their target audience and then complained that they didn't have enough seats filled. As one speaker confessed to me after complaining that no one was registering for her talk because she was promoting it to people outside of the target area. That confession and the frustration I felt in getting others to pull their weight changed how I work with speakers. Now I require each speaker to pay a registration fee of say $60 which is refundable if they have a minimum number of attendees for their talk. My reason for doing this is simple. Why should I pay for a room when it isn't being filled? In other words, if I've paid for the room and a speaker can't get 10 people to come to their talk then I'm still paying for the room that isn't being used (or underused) during that time. By the way if the speaker has 10 or more attendees then they get their $60 back.

D.   I also ask speakers to make an offer or at the very least have multiple products to sell at the event. One reason I always make money at each event is because I have multiple products to sell that attendees actually need. So whether it's a new book, a magazine subscription or a directory or advertising; I make money. I essentially make sure I give attendees an opportunity to say 'yes' very easily.

E.   I want you to make money. Another reason my events work is because I give speakers multiple ways to make money. While I never pay speakers (again would you pay a speaker that says they can fill seats then can't deliver?) all speakers can make an offer, which is how we make our money. Speakers also receive a copy of the attendee list including e-mails so that they can send a thank you to each attendee (and promote their other product and services). If you have 10 people attend your event and can't get one of them to purchase any of your products or services then there is a problem.

F.   Make that money. Okay so now that you have an e-mail list of attendees, you've got to stay on their radar. With a few exceptions, most attendees won't buy from you the first time. It's really about keeping your name in front of them so that they will eventually buy from you or attend a future event/workshop etc.

6.   One of the best ways to get paid regardless if your booking is a paid or non-paid gig is to get sponsors to pay you for speaking. And it's easier than you think. Let's say that you are giving a talk at your local Chamber. And just for the sake of argument the organization is expecting you to speak for free but will allow you to make an offer at the event. One way to get paid is to have the sponsor pay you in exchange for promoting their product to your audience. One advantage to underwriting my workshops is the fact that the sponsor gets a copy of the attendee list as well as the exposure.

How to get paid......

1. Opportunities like Experience Unlimited and SBA (Small Business Administration) are free talks only if you don't turn the appearances into revenue or another gig. In other words, part of the reason I never worry about taking on a pro bono gig is because I always turn it into revenue. So even "free talks" are turned into revenue and additional gigs because I walk out of each session with a list of e-mails/business cards from attendees and I send them info on upcoming events, workshops (paid) or additional gigs. The secret for me is to have many products and services to sell after the talk to make sure, one way or another, I get paid. Again this includes revenue from magazine subscriptions and advertising, booking services, book sales, mentoring programs, coaching, workshops and events. The more you have to offer attendees, the more likely you'll walk away from any "free" talk with revenue.

2. Another tip is to pepper any free event with people that can actually afford to pay you for your services or can book you into another gig. Last month alone I booked 4 speaking engagements while speaking at NAWBO (National Association of Women Business Owners) where I've booked several speakers and have turned 3 of them into return engagements for next year. This 1 gig turned into thousands in revenue thru the booking service the new directory for speakers (which comes out Dec. 15th 2015) and one on one coaching.

3. Media. So you've been booked on a number of media appearances but are you turning that appearance into revenue? Establishing yourself as a "go to" person is the key for getting more gigs. Case in point; CCSF(Community College of San Francisco) not only heard about me via a couple of media appearances and workshops I've done, but also because I have a rep in the business community of being well connected in political, celebrity and business circles. The result is an opportunity to speak at

CCSF for 4 weeks with a 50/50 split of revenue. This of course didn't happen overnight and took months of calls and e-mails, but once they did their research, CCSF was very eager to book me. Compliance Online http://complianceonline.com/ is another organization that hosts webinars and pays a minimum of $200 for a 90 minute talk or a percentage of the take whichever is higher. The great news is that not only do they pay you for that first webinar, but they also pay residuals. Compliance was another organization that heard about me because I sent them a recording of one of my media interviews. To date I'm still receiving residual income from the one webinar I conducted back in February of 2015. The bottom line is that the reason a speaker conducts a media interview to begin with is to get the word out about their products or service. But the way to use it is to get the audio, video, etc. into the hands of people that are likely to hire you (i.e. decision makers via a newsletter or e-mail) on your website, via social media.

4. What to do while waiting. Decision makers only book speakers when they have a need, a budget or a fit for that speaker. If they don't like what they see on the speaker sheet, they move on to the next speaker which means it can take a while before a speaker is booked. The best way to get more gigs is to have multiple topics to talk about. There's a reason I have over 30 topics to speak on and get booked to speak several times per month. If you look at my bio it's really a matter of when do they need me and am I a good fit? So what can you do while waiting? Simple. Create a webinar or workshop all your own which is less expensive than you might think. It's also another way to ensure that you're always speaking and generating revenue. For example Fort Mason Center in San Francisco rents rooms for approx. $31 per hour (prices vary) with a minimum of 3 hours. If you charge $99 per person for your workshop and only get 10 people (all speakers should be able to get at least 10 people to any event) you'll still turn a $897 profit for a 90 minute talk for a small group. If you host a webinar or teleseminar which costs virtually nothing to produce (except your time and energy) then you'll make an even bigger profit margin. Of course this doesn't include any offers or coaching fees (or additional gigs) you're likely to make after the talk. This method is why I always host several speaking engagements throughout the year and rarely worry about getting paid from any of them.

5. I always caution (and respect) speakers that may want to discontinue my booking service for lack of funds to always continue following up with leads I've already generated. The one mistake speakers make when leaving a lead generation program is to let hot leads go cold.

6. The bottom line is that you must work the leads and opportunities that are given to you. Strategize the best way to turn every appearance into revenue and you'll never worry about not making money from free speaking gigs

Be sure to pick up a copy of my directory of meeting planners
https://www.eventbrite.com/e/podium-magazines-big-book-of-professional-coaches-

I've written a lot about how to find speaking engagements. So much so that people often ask me to post some of my favorite resources, tips and websites etc. for finding gigs. Many of these can be found in my speakers Directory https://www.eventbrite.com/e/podium-magazines-big-book-of-professional-coaches-consultantsspeakersmeeting-planners-media-tickets-15821944863   but here's a list to get you started.

Chapter Eight: Who's hiring? Finding and creating new opportunities

The difference between speakers that make money and those that don't comes down to one word-opportunity. Below are some of my top tips for creating or finding opportunities to speak.

1.   Have a lead flow system in place ahead of time. Having a system in place will get you to manage your leads in a way that is efficient and cost effective. Think about it this way. How much time do you spend trying to remember every meeting planner and contact you've met in the last year? How do you know when to contact them? How do you track the type of speaker they're looking for and whether it's a paid gig or not? A lead flow system (i.e. Salesforce or A.C.T.) will help you manage those leads more efficiently so you can stay on top of when planners are booking speakers. Here's a great example, the SBA begins booking speakers for their San Francisco Small Business Week function (which is the second week in May) in Feb. They typically won't even entertain speakers until then and the organizers tend to book speakers they've worked with in the past before booking new speakers. I know this because I've been booked as a speaker/coach for the last few years.

2.   Meeting planners- One of the easiest ways to find people that plan and book events is to simply Google "Meeting Planners or Meeting Planners Association." But another way is to do a search for events on sites like Eventbrite.com, eventful.com and other event sites. Typically there is an e-mail address for the planner to submit proposals, one sheets etc. This is where you'll have to do a great deal of research but it's worth it. Make sure to visit the site of the event to see when they've booked speakers in the past so you can contact them next year.

3.   Public Speakers Association http://publicspeakersassociation.com/ run by Tonya Hofmann and a great resource for finding speaking opportunities. Dues range in price but it's worth every penny. What makes Tonya a valuable resource is the fact that not only does she help speakers find speaking opportunities thru her e-mail blasts but she also books speakers for events(both virtual as well as in person).

4.   Colleges and Universities- These are a bit more difficult but not impossible. For example CCSF.edu (City College San Francisco) books speakers/instructors on a regular basis. The link to register is https://www.ccsf.edu/en/educational-programs/contract-education.html . Many have honorariums and you must submit a proposal in order to be considered. Simply choose the college of interest to you and visit their website. Most have a call for speakers or instructors but you may need to dig a bit (always a good idea to call the school to inquire which department books speakers and instructors).

5.   Meetingnet.com –This is an online magazine that lists events as well as event planners

6.   Insightly.com - Another great resource is insightly.com which is primarily used as a CRM

7.   Benjibruce.com offers tips and resources to meeting planners and speakers.

8.   Hootsuite.com-Another great resource for finding meeting planners is Hootsuite.com which lists meeting planners

9.   One tip I always give to speakers is to always look for speaking opportunities where you are. Look at hotels that host conventions as well as convention centers. Find out who is speaking and then conduct some research to find out if they are booking speakers for the event. Many times a speaker will allow you to speak at their event if you are well connected and can help them fill seats.

10.   San Francisco Book of lists- So sometimes finding speaking gigs is as simple as looking up conventions. In San Francisco/Bay Area we have the San Francisco Book of Lists which is published annually by the San Francisco Business Times   . What most people don't know is that most major cities publish a business newspaper and directory. These will typically list the various conventions and convention centers for bookings.

11.   National Activity of Campus Activity Network

12.   Talkwalker.com

13.   Destination Management Companies-Handles bookings of speakers for clients.

14.   Sometimes you have to attend a few conferences to get booked at a conference. There's no better way than getting up close and personal to a planner at a conference to find out how to get booked as a speaker.

15.   Follow similar speakers on social media to find out where they're speaking and then book yourself at "appropriate" venues. Keep in mind that if you're relatively new to the speaking game it might be inappropriate to speak at a venue that just hosted a speaker that fills stadiums. Stay in your lane and don't deviate until you're ready.

16.   Speaking lifestyle.com- And click on the "resources" tab to see a list of speaking opportunities.

Chapter Nine: Why publishing a book (may) get you more gigs than not.

I received a call from a prospect today saying that she had just published her first book and wanted to hire me to book some media appearances for her. I decided to ask a few questions to determine the best way to help her. For example, does she have a one sheet? A press release? Is she a self-published author or did she go the traditional route? All are important questions because publishers/PR reps generally supply a press release if going the traditional path. If an author is self-published, then they must write the release themselves. The prospect mentioned that she had gone thru a self-publishing house and upon hearing this I asked her what she thought of the process (I secretly already knew what she was going to say). She said that it was a terrible experience and felt frustrated with the process and the fact that there were several people handling her account, none of them knew how to communicate with the other; not to mention the cost to produce the book. I then told her my story about how my first book (self-published) was thru a similar publishing house and that I experienced some of the same issues but that my other 3 books had gone thru Createspace.com which is owned by Amazon.com. And then I had to deliver the bad news. Createspace.com only charges authors for extra amenities like creating a customized book cover, otherwise the entire process is free. She mentioned that she remembered visiting the site but thought it was too good to be true so she went with her second option. The moral of the story is this. Do your research. Ask questions of your peers. Talk to friends that have published. The Internet makes it easy to find reviews and other information about a business that there is almost no excuse for making a blind purchase that will leave you dissatisfied as well as financially strapped.

Do I need to write a book to become a speaker?

I've always been a writer or at least I've always thought of myself as a writer. As far back as I can remember the desire to put my thoughts to paper has always been a part of my life.

I guess it started with my first play which I wrote, produced and directed in the 5th grade before I knew what any of those words meant. Because I've always been a little different (a shy child with a penchant for writing poetry and getting beat up) my world view has always been a bit...unique. So when I decided to write my first book on B2B telemarketing, it was no surprise that it subject matter didn't exactly set the literary community on fire. Nevertheless I was determined to publish come Hell or high water. And so I set out to find a publisher and an agent.

Six months later I was still trying to find someone who thought my book was good enough or marketable enough to publish. Of course that never happened. No market I was told. Who would buy a B2B book on telemarketing anyway? So after a few months of deliberation with myself I opted to self- publish (not that I had a choice). It's important to note that at this time (approx. 15 years ago) self-publishing was frowned upon by the literary community. It meant in a sense that you weren't good enough to be published traditionally. Nevertheless I decided to take a chance and publish in this format and see where it got me. My reasoning was that if I didn't publish then I would remain a consultant (nothing wrong with that). However if I published (even thru a Vanity press) then I would be known as an author as well as a consultant, which worked well for my brand. So I published my first book Telemarketing Success for Small and Mid-sized Firms which oddly enough became a best seller and the go to for anyone looking to launch a telemarketing campaign. Naturally this success gave me a sense of satisfaction given that every publisher in the industry at the time had rejected me. It also helped to launch my speaking career which was okay but nothing to write home about. To be honest my primary focus was coaching one firm at a time rather than hosting a workshop. So when the book was finally released I decided that in order to reach a different audience I would have to do things differently. That meant hosting workshops for my core audience of sales professionals and CEOs. Both the book and workshops were extremely successful garnering multiple invitations to coach or train sales teams around the globe.

One of my most successful speaking invitations came in the form of a regular reader of my column (which I also landed because of my book). The owner of a small but thriving janitorial firm "Jack" contacted me about flying to New York to (All expenses paid) to consult his team on the right way to make a sales call. This led to making NYC my part time home for approximately six months and prompted me to write my second book (The Single Person's Cookbook) as well as two more books (Surviving the economy and The Career Whisperer).

I guess what I'm saying is this. To publish a book is a great accomplishment and to be honest, I feel that everyone should experience it at least once to know what it feels like to publish. Does a speaker really need to publish a book in order to get speaking gigs? Not really. But there are some definite advantages.

1.   Publishing gives you instant credibility and increases your brand awareness. One of the reasons I decided to publish wasn't because I wanted to increase my brand awareness. What I was hoping to do was build my credibility as a coach by becoming an author. Keep in mind that my primary job at the time was as a high priced B2B telemarketer. I just wanted to be known as a writer, preferably one that made a living doing what he loved. But sometimes the universe just won't make things easy for you, in which case you need to create opportunities for yourself. It's not about breaking the rules but rather changing the rules you had nothing to do with creating.

2.   Publishing a book gets you more noticed a more often than not by event planners. When a planner is going over a speaker's one sheet to determine if they are a good fit for a booking, they're looking at several factors. Is the speaker local? What's their area of expertise? Can they fill a room? What's their topic and is it applicable to the audience? And are they published? Publication (as I mentioned earlier) gives speakers instant cred. So if a planner must choose between a speaker with a book to promote or a speaker without a book, then they will most likely go with the speaker with a book that speaks to the subject matter.

3.   Publishing doesn't always mean a book. There are many speakers that book tons of gigs who only have regular blog. Blogs are terrific if done correctly. That is to say that the content must be top notch and published on a regular basis and most importantly the content must be timely and searchable. That is to say that new readers must be able to find it via search engines. Publishing a regular blog (which can be turned into a book FYI) is a great way to get your message out to your target audience even if you're intimidated by the thought of publishing a book. It's sort of like book publishing but in smaller steps.

4.   Still not ready to publish a book but want more recognition? Consider submitting articles to a magazine for publication. This is a great way to add a byline or credit to your bio. Think about how great it would be to add "as seen in Huffington Post", to your bio.

Here's the thing. I know plenty of speakers that don't have a book a blog or a platform for getting the word out about their brand but still manage to book plenty of speaking gigs. Is it necessary to publish a book to land gigs? Not really, but it certainly helps.

Chapter Ten: The tools a good speaker needs to get hired

So what are event planners really looking for when booking speakers?

I decided to poll successful speakers, event planners and decision makers to get a clear understanding of what they're looking for and more importantly why some speakers book more gigs than others. Here's what they had to say…….

1.   Decision makers book speakers that fill rooms. Why would an event planner book a speaker that can't bring something to the table (i.e. fill seats)? This isn't necessarily about booking a well-known speaker, but rather a speaker with great content and presence.

2.   Meeting planners book Keynote speakers that command a minimum of $2500 per speech. I interviewed a number of top tiered speakers like Tonya Hofmann, Founder of Public Speakers Association and Jeff Hayzlett, MSNBC commentator to share their tips on making it as a speaker. What was surprising is that almost every one that I interviewed said almost exactly the same thing. Event planners won't take any speaker seriously that charges under $2500 per speech. To them it shows that they haven't been in the game long enough to command serious money.

3.   Event planners want to see the following….

A.   A one sheet that tells them who you are, what topics you can speak on and why they should book you. The one sheet should be just that, a one page that tells the planner who you are and why they need to book you ASAP. You always want to give the impression that you are a highly in demand speaker (even if you aren't). It should include a current picture and any topics that can speak on (as many as possible because the planner has a limited number of spots and unless you're a name, you want one of those spots to be yours).

B.   Speaker rates- This of course is optional in terms of putting it on your speaker sheet. Here's what's interesting. Having your rates on your sheet is sometimes a deterrent for bookings because a lot of planners see the fee and think automatically" I can't afford this speaker" and move on to the next speaker. So I'm not going to say that having your rates listed won't get you booked I'm just saying that planners tend to see what's in front of them. It's like knowing you have a free trip somewhere but have to pay the nominal sales tax. The thing most people will focus on isn't the free trip but the tax they have to pay.

C.   A current website and speaker reel- Most speakers already have a site but perhaps not a speaker reel. A speaker reel is a 10-20 minute video of you speaking in front of a live audience. It gives meeting planners an idea of your range and style of speaking. If you're booking speakers, wouldn't you want to see how good the speaker is?

Chapter Eleven: What to Expect Out of Your Speaker

I've mentioned Tonya Hofmann and/or Public Speakers Association http://publicspeakersassociation.com/ throughout this book and so I decided to solicit some advice for speakers from Ms. Hofmann who is the head of the PSA and the host of the popular Tonya Hofmann Internet TV Show https://www.youtube.com/channel/UCJFddKzvqH9_AneRKoE85jw . Here's what she had to say…

The market for speakers is always changing. All events, even virtual ones, are demanding and stressful, and need speakers to be a part of their success team rather than just flying in and out without much interaction. This article will explore how events can find creative ways to balance the investment in speakers with the end result: an informed, enlightened and motivated audience, as well as satisfied clients, sponsors, volunteers – and even the speakers themselves.

The Speaker's Mindset

In the past, speakers often had an "employee" mindset. Someone would contact a speaker, negotiate the fee and travel expenses, book the time and the topic, and then have little interaction until the event. With this approach, speakers are paid for their time and their expertise and rarely offer anything extra. The "employee" attitude is most common with celebrities, CEOs and sought-after speakers whose time is very limited.

These days most professional speakers have a more entrepreneurial mindset. Their goal is to create momentum and interaction, and their highest accomplishment at your event is to have done that well. Such speakers work with event organizers on marketing and promotion to help create excitement about the event, and are sometimes involved in attracting attendees, vendors, sponsors and even other speakers to achieve this goal. Well-delivered presentations at well-organized events earn the speakers name recognition, get their message heard, drive sales and opportunities, and build their reputation as forces for true change.

Speakers' Fees

Speakers' fees have changed along with the changing times. Everything seems to be negotiable in today's market. For both the speaker and the event, the challenge is to figure out how to create a win for both.

Speakers' fees range from $0 to thousands, but under certain circumstances even the most popular and sought-after speaker will speak for no or low fees nowadays. Working within your budget, you will have to decide how flexible you can be in your negotiations with prospective speakers. Open-minded and creative negotiations about fees can result in a fresh new approach that will benefit all parties. If your budget is low, you could supplement the speaker's fee with one or more of these other options.

There are some speakers that are just worth paying for. As I mentioned, the more in demand someone is the less time they have open on their calendar. To secure those who you want to absolutely speak at the event, agree up front on their speaker's fee. You can always throw in some of these other options for marketing benefits as an extra bonus offer for them to say "YES"!

The paid for speaker is a great marketing platform for your event. Make sure you utilize their name, head shot, bio, titles, videos, etc. to enhance your attendance package. If they are not as well-known but bring huge value on the training aspect, focus your marketing on the brilliance of the actual activity and presentation. Pump up your marketing to create a Wow environment so that the attendees are looking forward to the presentation.

Promotion

Speakers usually have large lists of contacts on social media and email marketing that can be utilized to drive more traffic to the event. Both the event and the speaker benefit from having more people to connect with. With careful negotiations, most speakers will be willing to do several things to help promote the event. They might send out social media posts, place the information in their email newsletter or even create a specific email about the event. Speakers can also give the attendees some things to prepare before the event so they will get more out of it at the time. Other possibilities include posting a banner or other event details on their website, handing out fliers or postcards at other events, and personally connecting with people who might want to attend or be a vendor or sponsor.

Writing a Blog

Speakers could be asked to write a blog or article for your next newsletter or website. This will bring more interest around the keynote presentation and any workshops or training at the event. After-conference blogs or articles will also continue the conversation and training.

Speakers' Availability

Attendees expect and appreciate more interaction before, during and after the event with those who are training, inspiring and motivating them. Greater speaker availability helps the retention of knowledge because it gives attendees opportunities to ask questions and discuss what they just heard. Speakers are usually happy to sign on for more interaction because they realize that being available to connect with the attendees is vital in today's market. Most speakers want to be there for questions, comments, interaction, conversation and other opportunities to connect. Today's professional speakers thrive on this approach, which gives them a sense of bringing significance to the events they speak at.

Pre/Post-Event Interaction

The payoff can be great when you entice the attendees, vendors and sponsors by introducing the speakers in advance. Speakers benefit by connecting with the crowd and warming everyone up to their message before the event. Simple audio or video calls can be recorded and posted on YouTube to create excitement for the event on your website, in newsletters and via social media connections. It is so easy for speakers to record a two- to five-minute video introducing themselves, talking about what they will be training on at the event, and encouraging people to attend. People love video and getting to hear a speaker's message beforehand. As a bonus, putting the videos on the conference website also helps with the website's search engine optimization because Google loves video!

After the event, sending a video or teleseminar offering a follow-up with the speakers will help ensure that the participants remember what they need to do, accomplish, take action on. The attendees will feel even more empowered and motivated, and will have immediate action plans to contribute to the follow-up meeting. This approach brings huge value to attendees and especially to corporate accounts that are looking for reasons to send their employees to an event.

Giveaways

Ask the speaker(s) to offer giveaways or special bonuses to attendees, sponsors and VIP guests. Suppose there are 10 workshop trainers and one keynoter, and each speaker gives away a special bonus to those who attend in person versus on a simulcast, or to those who sign up before a cut-off date. If each speaker offers a PDF, a promo item or a ticket to a special webinar, for example, and each one is worth $100, then you can promote a total value of more than $1,000 in bonus offers! This is a great strategy to get people to buy their tickets early, and again the speakers love it since the attendees get to know about them ahead of time.

Extras for VIPs/Volunteers/Sponsors

Speakers can also bring extra value to special marketing and promotions or to certain individuals. For a thank-you party for volunteers or at events for your VIP guests, sponsors, vendors, etc., speakers can do something special as a bonus – even an exclusive webinar/ teleconference call with your special guests. Most speakers would jump at the chance to speak more than once and it gives your organization another marketing approach to promote those VIP tickets or another reason for sponsors to jump in.

Vendor Booths and Sales

Many speakers want to sell products, sign books, offer a contest or giveaway for lead generation, and interact. Sometimes offering a booth or a table for such activities can be enough to reduce or even offset the speaker's fee. It might be necessary to negotiate the size of the area with the speaker to make sure the space is adequate. They could be bringing a sign or banner to hang, or they might need a chair or bar stool, room to do an activity, or skirting for a table – or they might prefer to be in your vendor, sponsorship or exhibit area.

No Sales

If you really don't want selling of any kind or any lead generation at your event, then you will need to pay the speakers for their time and higher speakers' fees will come into play. However, be careful, because audiences can get only so much from a 30-minute or even a two-hour presentation. If the audience is to learn some new ideas and skills and transform their habits, tactics, challenges, businesses, lives, etc., they must go further with the speaker to create permanent and lasting change – and that's a sales process. If sales are out of the question, then it might be necessary to buy some books from the speaker for the attendees, provide contact information for all the attendees, sponsors or vendors, or allow speakers to hand out contest forms, for example. Be creative in the sales approach if a "pitch" isn't something you want.

Revenue Sharing

Is your event a fundraising opportunity for your business, organization or company? Many speakers will consider revenue sharing, where they sell at your event and split the profit with you. If they offer something amazing on stage and/or at their booth, then they give the event a percentage; 25/75 or 40/60 splits are usual. (Lower amount to the event and higher to the speaker.) This could generate significant revenue for the event. Because you are providing the speakers with a venue for sales, prospective new clients, an atmosphere of excitement and a unique marketing opportunity, of course they will be pleased to give back.

Be Creative

Ideally most of these ideas would be negotiated into the speaker's contract, but at a minimum aim to include all the negotiable selections that you feel are essential for both the speaker and the event. This is the negotiation platform to start with. Most professional speakers will consider any and all of these options because in today's market there are plenty of amazing speakers to choose from and they will all want to participate in and contribute to a successful and effective event.

As an event organizer, the most effective utilization of a speaker is at the end of the event. It is the satisfaction that the whole event went off without a hitch. When the attendees, vendors, sponsors and speakers reach out to tell you what an amazing event it was for them. That moment of complete satisfaction is the outcome that everyone is searching for. I learned a long time ago, you don't know what you can get until you ask but if you never ask, you never get. So discuss your expectations, desires and ultimate outcome you wish to create and most people are on the same platform with you. Most people want to help to achieve your goals because truthfully, it is usually their goals too. When goals are aligned, then the outcome is inevitable. If the speaker has completely different goals than you do, it is better to find someone else so that the outcome is achievable. Most importantly, have fun! Life is too short to deal with mean, grumpy or negative people and there are way too many amazing, incredible and nice people on this planet to deal with anyone who isn't just plan FABULOUS!

I know that I love not only speaking and putting on my own events but especially helping create a success for someone else in their business and in their life. Always look for the person who will continue to grow, collaborate, connect and help you achieve your goals!

 Tonya Hofmann is the CEO/Founder of the Public Speakers Association. www.PublicSpeakersAssociation.com and www.TonyaHofmann.com

Chapter Twelve: Media Tips

Business and Media: Part One- The who, what, where and how of getting your message out to the world...

You've built a solid reputation in the business community. You're services are selling well within your immediate sales territory. But now you're thinking globally and have to get the word out to the rest of the world. But there's one problem. You don't know where to start or who to contact to create a buzz on an international level. So I'm going to give you my top tips for generating word of mouth for your business. Everything from the basics of writing and sending press releases to who to send them to and how to get booked in the media (it's easier than you might think).

1.   Press releases- Sending a press release is your way of letting the world know that you have a new product, service or other business announcement. However sending a compelling press release (while tricky) to the media is in some ways as simple as writing a letter. Here's the trick. According to Small Business PR (http://www.smallbusinesspr.com/pr-learning-center/diagrams-templates/press-release-template.html) there are several rules to writing an effective release.

NEWS RELEASE TEMPLATE

1. Headline: Get readers to click on the link to the story. (social, search, etc.) Write the headline you want to see on the article in a targeted publication and write a headline that is interesting enough to tweet.

2. Head: Entice reader to consume content. Sub-head adds more detail to the headline.

3. Dateline: Includes the city of origin, and the date of the release.

4. Lead Sentence: Lead paragraph starts with an interesting statement, not boilerplate.

5. CALL TO ACTION: Most readers won't make it to the bottom of the page. Insert your call to action link for the public after the first or second paragraph

6. Copy Body: Tell the story. This is your hook which tells the reader why they should keep reading.

7. Media contact info: Establish the brand's credentials and give journalists the about-the-company details they need for the story.

8.   Press release distribution- According to http://www.avangate.com these are some of the top FREE PR distribution services. Sending out a press release can cost up to $300 a pop which can get pretty

pricey. So the key here is to find the ones that offer the service for little or no money. Here's a list to get you started.

1. http://www.npr.org/

2. http://www.betanews.com

3. http://www.directionsmag.com

4. http://news.thomasnet.com/

5. http://www.nanotech-now.com

6. http://www.prlog.org/

7. http://www.downloadjunction.com

8. http://www.newswiretoday.com/

9. http://www.pr-inside.com/

10. http://www.24-7pressrelease.com

11. http://www.pr.com/

12. http://www.prleap.com/

13. http://www.free-press-release.com/

14. http://www.clickpress.com/

15. http://www.pressbox.co.uk/

16. http://www.filecluster.com/

17. http://digitalmediaonlineinc.com/

18.   http://www.onlineprnews.com/

19. http://www.i-newswire.com/

20. http://www.cgidir.com/

21. http://www.przoom.com/

22. http://www.openpr.com/

23. http://www.sbwire.com/

24. http://www.1888pressrelease.com/

25. http://www.theopenpress.com/

26. http://www.free-press-release-center.info/

27. http://www.prfree.com/

28. http://www.ukprwire.com/

29. http://www.itbsoftware.com/

30. http://www.itbinternet.com

31. http://www.freepressreleases.co.uk/

32. http://freepressindex.com/

33. http://www.prwindow.com/

34. http://www.prurgent.com/

35. http://www.freepressrelease.com.au/

36. http://www.afreego.com/

37. http://pressabout.com/

38. http://www.pressmethod.com/

39. http://pr-gb.com/

40. http://www.pressexposure.com/

41. http://www.mediasyndicate.com

42. http://prmac.com/

43. http://www.publicitywires.com/

44. http://www.seenation.com/

45. http://www.afly.com/

46. http://www.addpr.com/

47. http://www.pressreleasecirculation.com/

48. http://jkhanok.com/

49. http://news.eboomwebsolutions.com/

50. http://emeapr.com/

Haro.com - Help a reporter out (Haro get it?) is an online forum designed to connect journalists from around the world with industry experts. Simply register (for free) with the site and you'll instantly begin receiving e-mails listing a variety of media opportunites. These include (but not limited to) health and beauty, fitness, business, lifestyle. Once you're in the system, you'll begin to receive notices 3 times a day. Just choose the listing you want to apply to, follow the instructions and submit. Be warned, hearing back from a journalist may take up to 30 days or more.

If you're a journalist looking for stories it makes sense to submit a query as well.

Google plus, Twitter, Pinrest,Linkedin.com and Facebook-Truth be told I was slow to register with these staples of social media. It took the launch of my radio show in 2011 to even consider using social media to promote anything. Thank goodness I did because it helped get the word out (about my show) exponentially and in a very short time. I prefer using these sites for different purposes. For example, I use all 5 platforms to promote my magazine however I use only Googleplus, Twitter and Facebook when I want to give my audience a visual of the latest issue. I use Linkedin.com for increasing subscriptions and ad sales and Facebook for promoting different events (via Eventbrite).

Meetups- I really like meetups because they are topic/genre specific. For example if you're in the culinary industry and looking to promote to the food industry, simply search food groups on the site and you'll see all of the food meetups in your area; great for meeting and promoting to like-minded people.

Linked in.com is the Facebook of business social media. And while I've listed it in the section above, it bears repeating because quite a number of people (still) aren't aware of it or never use it. Here's why you need to take a second look. Not only is 'LI 'good for finding work, it's a great resource for everything from webinars and blogs to local events. One question you're likely to hear at a networking event is whether or not you're on Linkedin.com. If the answer is no, then I'd suggest creating a profile ASAP. Trust me; it's imperative to building your professional brand.

Huffington Post/Examiner.com and Allbusiness.com- These 3 sites are terrific for the writer looking to gain some international exposure while earning a few bucks. What I liked about blogging for such established sites is the "brand boost "associated with writing for a high profile and well established site. Writing for an established site means that while you'll still need to promote your blog, your brand receives a boost simply by writing for the site. Of the 3 sites, Allbusiness.com is the only one that pays its writers a small regular monthly stipend. The other 2 are mostly pay per click which is fine if you're just looking for brand exposure. But if you're looking to pay your rent then keep looking. Want proof that sites like these are worth your time? When I was writing for Allbusiness.com I was contacted by a Manhattan based small business owner looking to increase his sales team's close ratio. This business owner requested a consulting quote which I sent along with basic info on my services and excerpts from my book. Not only did he hire me for a long term consulting gig, he also put me up in a four star hotel, paid for my flight and bought copies of my book(in addition to paying my consulting fee). This exchange led me to a six month commute (I love NYC) to and from NYC and a $500 a month sublet in Harlem. And while living in NYC, I promoted my second book, The Single Person's Cookbook www.amazon.com and wrote the draft for my first film The Mo Diaries www.amazon.com ;all because of a little blog on www.allbusiness.com. The moral of the story? Just because a low paying or pro bono opportunity presents itself doesn't mean that it won't pay big dividends in other ways. As long as you're getting the results you want keep at it and the profits will come.

Youtube/Ustream.com/ Livestream.com/Animoto.com/Blab.ie/Periscope- Want to host your own online TV show? Consider videotaping and posting your own segments online for your audience (and the world) to see. Youtube has become so synonymous with online viewing that more than 50% of Americans have gotten rid of their cable and now watch TV online (yours truly included). Ustream and Livestream are essentially the next generation of online TV viewing and streaming. Although you won't see popular TV shows like Modern Family on these sites, you will see original programing (most of it live). And best of all, uploading a 30 minute program costs absolutely nothing.

Animoto.com has become a lifesaver of sorts for me because it allows me to edit video footage and add music and content in a few easy steps and all for a monthly subscription cost of $39.00.

Blogtalkradio.com-Interested in hosting your own radio show? Then Blogtalkradio.com is for you. While there are a number of online options, Blogtalkradio.com is the gold standard with over 2 million shows on the site. Producing a half hour show costs you nothing (just a bit of pre-production)and is as simple as knowing which buttons to push. However, I highly recommend upgrading (over time) for as little as $39.00 per month. Still not convinced? Deepak Chopra has a show on the network. Good enough for him. Good enough for me.

Blab and Periscope- Both sites have become the next wave of online marketing for anyone looking to create visual content to sell books, host a webinar or just reach a whole new audience.

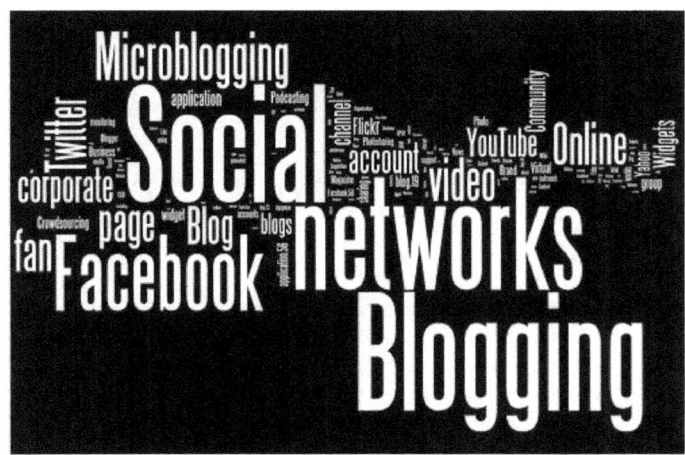

Business & Media: Part 2 Bookings 101

Here's everything you need to know about booking yourself on just about any media platform. The tips listed are primarily for Internet bookings but quite a few of the rules are applicable for traditional media as well…..

1. Radio- Getting booked on the radio is much easier than it was once upon a time. As a matter of fact it's easier to get booked on radio than just about any other media platform (easier but not easy).Because Internet radio is still a relatively new medium the rules are a bit more lax than say booking yourself on Howard Stern. The truth of the matter is that the more popular the show (i.e. Howard Stern) the more difficult it is to get booked without a top notch agent. Rather than trying to get booked on a big name show, instead focus on the smaller or local markets. For example……

   Blogtalkradio.com which has over 2 million shows on its network in a variety of topics. Most hosts/Executive producers handle their own bookings; which means it's really a matter of sending a simple query directly to them via the site itself. Don't turn your nose up at Internet radio because it's fast becoming the #1 media platform for obtaining publicity. However be warned that every show has its own rules for bookings. For example, I tend to book about 3 months (or more) in advance for my show.

2. Whether radio or TV; don't make your query too long(about a paragraph will do it). Include your contact info and suggest a topic of discussion or key talking points to cover.

3.   Make sure to listen to the show before you query; even a few minutes of listening to a program will give you a feel for the format. If it's not for you –move on.

4.   Be sure to note in your query that you've listened to a few shows and be prepared to site which episodes. This rule is true for *all* media.

5.   Do not send questions (when you get booked) unless the host has asked for it. A major pet peeve of mine is when a guest sends questions despite the fact that I've asked them not to(many show producers hat this as well and it's a great way to ensure that you won't be asked back). I tend to do my own due diligence and know direction I want the interview to go.

6.   Promote your segment. Part of the reason you're booked on a show is because you're bringing something to the show. Nothing frustrates a producer more than booking a guest that won't self-promote. Why would a producer re-book a guest with low ratings (from the first booking)? So the rule of thumb is to make sure to get the word out about your segment (be sure to let the producer know(in your query) that you'll help promote it too) via social media, e-mail and word of mouth.

7.   Traditional radio- It's a bit more difficult to get booked on a traditional station than it is Internet radio –but not impossible. Follow the rules listed above with one exception. Start with local shows and then move up to the larger markets. Again, do your research before reaching out to the booking agents/producers. Most of the contact info can be found on the show's website.

8.   Guest Blogs- Not ready to start your own blog? No problem. Guest blogging is more prevalent than you think. Simply do your research and query the blogger about accepting guest posts. Google for a list of sites that accept guest blog posts.

9.   Print- As always; conduct your research. Many columnists list their contact info on their site and they're always looking for story ideas. Pitch an idea that's topical and will generate a buzz.

10.   TV- One of the most difficult mediums for bookings but like everything else it just takes time ,patience and research to break through the barrier. When I got booked on The View from the Bay (Channel 7-local show) it was because I put a plan in motion that was designed to improve my chances of getting booked. First I found out who was in charge of bookings for the show. Second, I sent the booking agent a press release a bio and pitch ideas. Next, I got tickets to sit in the audience (tickets are free) after the show I walked up to the hosts for an autograph and asked a simple question. "Did you get the info on my new cookbook"? Spenser Christian (a true gentleman) replied that he hadn't but gave me the name of one of the other producers of the show and suggested I contact her about getting booked. One month later I appeared on the show for the first of 3 cooking segments to promote my cookbook-The Single Person's cookbook. This strategy wouldn't have worked for say, The Wendy Williams Show (they book celebrities mostly) but a local show will book based on subject matter-not celebrity.

Starting an Internet radio show. Steps to launching your new career as a radio host

I never intended to launch a career as a radio host. Despite the fact that all of my friends felt sure that this was the right path for me I didn't get it. I don't have the right voice for it. I'm impatient and technology isn't exactly a friend of mine. And yet here I am nearly 5 years into a career as a radio host with 200,000+ listeners worldwide and more advertisers than guests per show. The show has become so popular that I'm often asked how I got started in broadcasting. I've even created a successful workshop series around the subject matter. The reasons for starting your own show may vary, but the main reason is (or rather should be) to give yourself a regular –platform to establish your brand as an expert in your field. So here are my tips for launching your own career as well as the lessons I've learned along the way.

My journey….

First you should know that launching a career as a radio host is a LOT of work. It's about producing a quality show that people will tune in to on a regular basis. It's building a reputation that is self-sustaining regardless of if you're on hiatus for a few weeks or on the air live. It's walking into a networking event and at least 50% of the room already knows who you are and what you do (yes being a bit of a personality is both a blessing and a curse). It's about building a brand and a reputation for quality.

I had no intention of going into radio mostly because I didn't think I had the talent or temperament for it. It never even occurred to me until I was asked by another host on the same network to be a guest on her show. When she stood me up (twice) with one lame excuse after another, it got me to thinking of alternative ways to get the word out about my work. So as pissed off as I was about being blown off (twice-I'm just saying) I decided to launch my own radio show to take more control over how I got my message out. But who'd listen? What time would it be on? How would I promote it? And would anyone tune in to someone giving advice on business issues in an (at that point) untested platform like Internet radio? And then I got an idea….

No such thing as bad promotion

So after a lot of sleepless nights I decided that I was in fact ready to launch my show. I would call it Small Business Forum Radio (boring and unoriginal I know (it's my show so I can call it what I want to and it was the only name that didn't give me gas). I launched my new show on July 15th 2011 with a whopping 100 listeners the first month. Because I tend to get panic attacks when working on a new project I decided to ease my anxiety by booking people I knew (lesson #1-book people you know first to ease into any new forum) as my first guests. The show went surprisingly well and what's more I didn't need a shot of (Pearl) vodka to get thru it (who knew)? By the way, that first few shows I screwed up royally by cutting off guests, making noise in the background ,going off topic. I was a bit of a mess; but I got thru it, the more I did the show; the more comfortable I became. And what I learned was A) Unexpected things will happen on a live show B) Some booked guests will flake out and leave you with dead air C) Fifteen minutes is a Long time (to bomb) to fill when your guests do flake out so it's important to have a

D) Backup plan or filler to make sure you don't sound like a complete idiot. I also feel that knowing and anticipating that things will go wrong on a live show will make hosting and producing a successful show less stressful. Here are some other tips for creating a successful show.

1.   If you're hosting a talk format, be sure to ask your guests to help promote their segment (to their target audience) which establishes their credibility and in turn helps promote your show.

2.   Issue a query thru Haro.com to help you find guests for your show instead of sending out a mass e-mail. My first query garnered some 250 responses-within 48 hours.

3.   Know what your strengths and weaknesses are. For example, I'm really good at the interview and love researching topics, but I am horrible at chit chat when I have no one to engage. Which is why timing your guests appropriately is important

4.   Find a way to monetize your show thru advertisers or sponsors. Even bartering can help support your program via services or products you'd ordinarily have to pay for.

5.   Promote your show often and look for as many opportunities to get the word out as possible via speaking engagements, networking events and partnerships.

Launching an Internet radio show has opened numerous doors for me including, speaking engagements, revenue, comped tickets to select events, even free food and alcohol. But I think what I enjoy most about what I do is the fact that I can educate my audience and share the stories of my guests. And promoting small business is always a good thing.

How to use the media to generate business

I'm always amazed when clients complain that media interviews never generates immediate new business (but still book them anyway). Here's where speakers that feel this way are missing the boat. Media interviews are your calling card to garner more speaking gigs and are particularly useful if you aren't yet a name brand. Even if you are a Jeff Hayzlett who doesn't exactly need the publicity (since he has a top rated show and is a frequent contributor on MSNBC not to mention a best-selling author, speaker and a business associate of Donald Trump-don't hold that against him) he will still make the rounds and appear on shows like mine (Small Business Forum Radio www.blogtalkradio.com/tonywilkins)because he understands that any time you can get your name out to your target audience (in as many different forums as possible) is a good thing because it keeps your name front and center. Why do you think Donald Trump rarely spends money on advertising and promotion, even on his presidential campaign? It's because he understands that any time he does anything, it generates news so why spend money on advertising when he doesn't need to? Media isn't designed to necessarily generate sales for you (although it can if done properly). It's really designed so that when your name is brought up people know who you are. By keeping your name front and center of your target audience, you build your brand. It's as simple as that. Here are some tips for keeping your name front and center

First the why….

1.   Email your target audience when you're about to be interviewed. It's FREE publicity folks. So why wouldn't you contact your target audience to let them know you have information and tips to share with them. You're the expert and isn't part of being a speaker sharing information and knowledge with your target audience? It's also a great way to establish yourself as the expert in your field.

2.   Social media is your friend so be sure to post any new interviews on Linkedin.com, Facebook, Twitter, etc.

3.   Ask others to share your interview with people they know. There's nothing wrong with asking others to help spread the word about how fabulous you are.

4.   Make sure that a link of the interview is on your site.

5.   If you're helping to promote the media interview and the interviewer liked what you had to say chances are they will invite you for a follow up provided you help promote their platform.

6.   E-mail the link to event planners and ask if you can give a similar talk at their next event.

7. Ask the media personality if they are booking other guests and make recommendations based on their need. This makes you an invaluable resource and typically leads to a re-booking.

Media Matters: How to turn your next media appearance into revenue

Whether you're a seasoned speaker or new to the game, inevitably you'll need some media exposure. However getting booked on a radio show and using the exposure to generate revenue are two different things. Here are some tips for keeping your name in the public eye and using that exposure to generate more business.

"I don't need media exposure for my business". If you're a serious speaker you're going to need some exposure. Any time a meeting planner looks you up on Google, they're going to want to see what you've done. What groups have you spoken in front of? Have you spoken at any conventions or in the media? What did you talk about? Was you're appearance as a guest blogger or on a podcast? When someone searches your name only to find that you don't have any appearances or speaking gigs under your belt, it sends a message that you're not worth booking. And why should they? So the first step is to get booked on some well -established media platforms. My buddy Steve Caldwell of Manager Mojo www.managermojo.com is always on the lookout for people to interview and is one of the best interviewers out there. My show Small Business Forum Radio www.blogtalkradio.com/tonywilkins has nearly 200,000 listeners globally and books business owners months in advance. Try to get booked on shows that have a decent number of listeners, typically anything over 100,000 is good. Save the newer media platforms for "practice runs" to get comfortable talking to the media. Think of it as a training ground to get you ready for the next level.

"I contact media platforms all the time and no one ever gets back to me".

Here's the thing. You have to make an interesting case for someone to book you. One trick I use to get booked on a regular basis is to simply send a query or bio to see if/when media personalities are booking guests. The bio alone is impressive enough by itself and offers a brief description of my accomplishments. The hardest part is the waiting. If they really want you and need to fill a slot (say within 60 days) then they will get back to you sooner rather than later; but it isn't a guarantee. If you've sent out multiple queries and still don't hear back then it's time to re- think what you're sending out and to whom. Is it the right target audience? How often do they book similar guests? What's important to note is that media personalities receive requests on an almost daily basis. So much so that they begin to delete requests that don't immediately grab their attention. So the trick is to make yourself stand out and indispensable. I recently reached out an author who was writing a book on San Francisco CEOs. His assistant contacted me about the interview after receiving my query via HARO.COM (Help a reporter out) and promptly booked me for the interview. Two days later I received a phone call from the man himself expressing his thanks for the interview and requesting a one on one. The purpose (as I had already guessed) was to get booked on my radio show to promote his book which I naturally obliged. But while I had him on the phone I decided to use this new connection to my (and my client's) advantage. So I asked if he was open to booking other business owners for interviews. Of course he said "yes".(Why wouldn't he?) Note: I asked if he was "open" instead of "interested". It's a subtle but important difference. Asking if someone is open rather than interested will get you a yes more often than not. It's a psychological thing because it's harder to say "no I'm not open to that".

I've done multiple media interviews; none have turned into anything useful".

I get this complaint all the time and the short answer is that the person is using the media the wrong way. Simply going on radio or TV without promoting it to your core audience is a definite waste of time and resources. See, most people receive an invitation to be interviewed and think about their 15 minutes of fame instead of expanding to 30 days of fame which is what you want. The best way to use the media to your advantage is to promote the Hell out of it on social media, via newsletters, associations, and business groups and e-mail blasts to your target audience. This is your chance to shine. And here's the thing; promote it multiple times throughout the month. In fact get others to help spread the word to their network, which helps extend your 15 minutes exponentially.

"I'm thinking of starting my own Internet radio show to generate revenue and spread my message to others. How do I get started?"

Okay this is going to be a rather long and detailed explanation but here goes (the condensed version of course). And yes, this is how I launched a successful radio program.

Step one-Choose a name; which sounds simple enough but trust me it's more difficult to do this than you think. I went thru hundreds of possible names before I settled on the rather simplistic Small Business Forum Radio. Nothing I tried before seemed to fit. It was either too wordy or too pedantic or just plain stupid. Nothing seemed to work until I really thought about it. My goal in creating the show was to develop a forum for small business owners to educate my listeners on their area of expertise while promoting their work to the masses. So the name Small Business Forum Radio (and later magazine) just made sense. You also want to create name /brand recognition for the long haul so choose a name you can live with indefinitely.

Step two-Choose a time that works for you and is consistent. The mistake many new Internet radio hosts make is the same one that TV programmers make. If no one knows when you're going to be on, no one will know when to tune in; so choose a date and time and stick with it. You also want to be in charge of every aspect of producing your show from booking and interviewing guests to marketing. I've had guests ask if they can call in to my show at their convenience as if I'm doing nothing else in my life but waiting to interview them. Scheduling random interviews makes it a podcast rather than an Internet radio show and trust me, there *is* a difference. Podcasts are generally recorded interviews done pretty much at the discretion of the interviewer. Internet radio shows on the other hand are live shows that eventually wind up in the archive. I also have partners and advertisers just like traditional radio which isn't generally the case with podcasts. Ironically 90% of my listeners tune in after I'm off the air but I like the consistency of being on the air at a certain time. And by the way, my show remains in the archives in perpetuity which means that my guests and advertisers receive exposure forever.

My show airs LIVE Friday's at 3:30 Pm Pacific and then goes into the archives in perpetuity (more on why this important later) which makes it easy for my listeners to find me and tune in. This should not be confused with booking a segment for a podcast which is different than booking an Internet radio show.

Step Three- Call for guests- Finding guests won't be difficult but it doesn't mean that you won't have to get the word out that you're looking. Here's the thing. One of my initial worries was that no one would tune in. But what I forgot was that everyone wants their 15 minutes. And more importantly small business owners want (and need) to tell their stories because mainstream media wasn't (and still doesn't). So my show offers a platform that wasn't readily accessible to the average small business owner. How did I garner guests? I initially posted on Reporter Connection which no longer exists. But I also put the word out with my contacts, and on social media. What's interesting is that in 48hours I had over 250 business owners vying for a spot on my show. Years later we now have nearly 150,000 listeners globally and book 90 days in advance.

Step Four-Choose your guests-very carefully. As I found out the hard way, picking the wrong guests especially in the beginning can be detrimental to your burgeoning radio career. When booking guests you want to look for those that are first of interest to you and second of interest to your listeners. Why did I choose myself first? Because there is nothing more boring or tedious than booking someone on your show who bores you to tears (it happens). And when that happens it comes through in the interview. Your voice tells all, as do your mannerisms and that yawn in between questions. Here's a secret, if you ever tune in to my program and I don't ask a guest to come back at the end of the interview then you know I was bored. Sometimes you think a guest will be dynamic but once they get on the air they're as dull as dirt. Some people freeze when they go on the air because they think they have to memorize facts and figures in order to be interesting. I have a few rules. I never ask a guest a question they can't answer and I never send questions ahead of time. The reason is that I want my guests to have a simple conversation with me and nothing more. And because I'm such a skilled interviewer I try to make my guests feel very comfortable. So much so that many guests reveal that they were having such a great time that the 15 minutes went by too quickly.

Step Five- Do your due diligence. Write your preliminary questions. Schedule your show ahead of time. Confirm your guests. Here's the thing. Producing a live show every week takes a lot of time and energy and commitment. In the beginning (and I can't believe I'm admitting this) it took me days to produce a show. That meant booking the guests, confirming them, building the show platform on the site, promoting the show, recording promos, writing my questions, researching guests and finally launching the show. In the beginning it was a lot of work; now I have it down to a science and can get everything done in a matter of a couple of hours, which originally took me days. One of the great things about producing my show is the fact that I tend to conduct my own research which generally means that I reject questions from guests (I really hate when guests send questions ahead of time). I'm at the point where I actually delete these questions without looking at them. To me it's like a guest saying "interview me and here's what I want you to ask". Scheduling your audio and video and promos ahead of time will save you time in the long run. In fact I tend to book everything a few weeks prior and then delete if someone cancels. Once everything is ready to go I send an e-mail confirmation about a week prior and ask each guest to confirm the Wednesday before the interview (which is on Friday). If I don't hear from them by the end of business day Wednesday then I delete them from the program. It's important to be diligent about this because some people will be lame and wait until the last minute to confirm (which can stress you out because you've got to come up with filler (more on this later). Others will tell you that they forgot or got the time wrong or their cat had syphilis or... you get the point. Here's the thing. Stuff happen, but if it isn't important enough to put on your calendar then it's not important to re-schedule. If you treat your show as a business, guests will too.

Step Six- Breathe. You'll be fine. It's okay to be perfectly imperfect and make mistakes. My first year on the air was fraught with mishaps. I can laugh at all of them now but back then I worried over every little thing. The volume was wrong or the guests were boring or I didn't ask the right questions. I worried about everything including whether or not anyone would actually tune in to my show (in hindsight I was a complete idiot but whatever). Here's the thing about doing anything that's unfamiliar. You eventually figure it out. It's very easy to get caught up in the moment and lose your center. What you're about to accomplish is huge and can have an enormous impact on your business and brand not to mention the listeners and your guests, if done right. Do not underestimate the contribution you're about to make because it will be worth all the stress and effort.

Step Seven –The interview. This is where you shine. Everything you've done to ensure a successful broadcast happens here. The interview is when you show the type of interviewer you really are. Every radio producer has his or her own style. Some (like myself) prefer to write down preliminary questions ahead of time to keep focused and on track. While others like my buddy Valerie Branch who has her own show, prefers to interview off the cuff. The point is that you have to find your own style. One reason I prefer to write preliminary questions down is that it helps me to focus and remain in control. Since I'm not great at idle chit chat this technique has proven invaluable. It's important to note that while I do write down preliminary questions; my main focus is to have a casual chat with my guests. This means that while I may have my questions written down I always ask follow up questions which aren't written down. I'm going to be really frank here. This takes some skill and not everyone can make that kind of transition easily or successfully so don't be alarmed if your first few interviews are clumsy and awkward. You'll eventually get it.

Step eight- Filler. This is a separate step because this is the stuff no one tells you. "Filler" is what you need when your guest either forgets to call in or calls in late. In the beginning of my radio career guests would flake out on me at least once a month (it rarely happens now because most know that I take this behavior seriously). Guests would often state that they forgot they were booked to be on the show (despite receiving confirmations from me). Or worse ,they would tell me that they were "busy" which never works for me since we're all busy. Again if it isn't important enough to write it down then it isn't important enough to re-book you when you flake. When a guest cancels or flakes out you need "filler" which is essentially a list of topics to talk about until your guest shows or until your next guest calls in. This can also be music, news of the day, whatever. I'm not good at filler because I tend to ramble and it just comes off as unfocused and, well stupid. Luckily these days I can go to commercial instead of using filler. But back to my point, filler is important to have on hand because when someone does flake or calls in late (and trust me, it will happen), you have a significant amount of time to fill. Filling 5 minutes of dead air may not sound like a lot of time but you'd be amazed at how too much dead air will kill your show.

Step Nine-After the interview. So now that you've conducted your first interview and have wiped the sweat from your brow, it's time to make the most of it. I have a few rules for interviewing people. The first rule is that they have to be interesting. But more importantly they have to help promote their segment. This is infinitely important for growing your listenership as well as generating revenue because now you have a platform for educating your target audience (as do your guests) as well as a way to track your shows success. Send guests of your show a link and ask them to help spread the word. Twitter,Linkedin.com and Facebook as well as e-mail marketing to their target audience is a great way of getting the word out.

Step ten- Cashing in

Here's where the money comes in.

1.   Send a link to your target audience to get them to tune in. Educating your target audience or rather offering useful information to your core is one of the best ways for promoting yourself as an expert.

2.   Start booking advertisers to help supply you with income. One of the best things I did was figure out that small business owners are willing to pay to get the word out about their product/service provided you have the listeners to back it up. One of my smarter moves was waiting until I had over 10,000 listeners before I approached potential advertisers. If you're a business show be sure to reach out to your community and be aware that as an Internet radio show the entire world is your market.

3.   Once you've built an audience, let others (looking to launch their own show) know that they can build their own audience by being a regular guest host on your show. For example, I charge a monthly fee for 4 spots on my show (at the end of the show). This allows the guest -host to piggyback off of my established listenership while they build their own audience and credibility.

4.   Teach workshops- Once you've established yourself as a personality then it's time to teach or write about what you know. The market to give talks or give workshops to teach others how you've built a successful media platform is huge. Be sure to cash in.

5.   Write books- This is an opportunity to write about what you know and promote yourself as an expert and author. Remember authors make their money primarily on speaking gigs not on residuals.

Step Eleven: Marketing

Marketing is important because now that you have a platform you must promote it. There's nothing worse than having a great show that no one knows about. Get others to help promote it. Promote it via social media and go on other shows to promote it. I also recommend promoting your show via business groups on FB, meetups etc. Don't forget to let others know in your newsletter etc. One of my best strategies for promoting my show is to get public relations reps to do it for me. When a rep has a client that wants to promote their new book, they try and get them on as many shows as possible. Once that happens they work tirelessly to get others to tune in to their client on your show. It's like hiring a PR rep without having to pay them.

Got something more to say? Start your own magazine to promote your show and your magazine. When SBFR began generating both revenue and listeners I decided that it was time to launch a magazine to help promote my guests and my show in a way that goes beyond a 1 hour format. SBFM (Small Business Forum Magazine was launched 3 years ago and is promoted to over 40,000 business owners globally. We have advertisers and promoters that help get the word out which has expanded my brand exponentially.

Step Twelve-The price of fame.

Fame is a tricky thing. I never intended to be a radio personality. Heck I never intended to go into radio to begin with. But here I am with a successful media platform and tons of fans. The price of fame is that I've lost a bit of my autonomy (not much but a bit). And whenever I go to a networking event, people already know who I am which means that they inevitably want to get booked on the show. The good news is that I no longer have to beg people to come on my show. No longer have to convince others to advertise with me and no longer deal with flakey guests. The bad news is that it can be a bit overwhelming (not to mention difficult) to get away from the "Tony Wilkins" persona. It's not I'm suddenly this international celebrity. It's just that now-a-days I tend to shy away from telling people that I host a show(ironic huh?) because I never know if the person is interested in me or just wants some publicity. It can be a bit daunting to enter a networking event and find that nearly ½ the room knows you and wants your attention. Case in point I recently attended a networking event and before I could make my way to the bar I was introduced to a number of people all vying for my attention. It's flattering sure, but it can be a bit overwhelming at times. But the truth is that I am grateful for all of the support and attention the show receives. Life is good.

5 ways to raise brand awareness and generate revenue

As with most business owners, I'm always looking for ways to increase my brand awareness and revenue. And while some strategies have worked better than others over the years, here are some tried and true ways for building a brand and generating revenue.

1.   Teach what you know. This is probably my # 1 rule for raising brand awareness and generating revenue. Not everyone is cut out to command six figure speaking fees but that doesn't mean you can't put together an educational seminar that gets you noticed. For example, The Learning Annex.com is always looking for speakers to book. They handle the marketing and set up costs (booking the room) while taking a small percentage of the door. If you're not looking to give anyone a cut of your sales then simply find a venue that can accommodate anywhere between 25 or more attendees. Initially I think you should start small; say 25 people and then build up to selling out rooms of 100 or more. This way you're not overwhelmed with trying to speak to 200 people your first time out. Here are some steps to setting up your first speaking engagement.

· Everyone has something to say. So what's your message? In other words, is your message something the audience can relate to?

· Have talking points to keep you on point and hold the attention of the attendees. It's not as easy as you think considering that you have to engage them for 90 min or more. So staying on topic with great content is key to hosting a great seminar. Ask yourself what talking points are of most interest to the audience (not you) and why?

· Who is your audience? Before you can speak to an audience, you must first know who your audience is. Are you speaking to women owned business owners? Minority owned business owners? Unemployed people?

· Names, names, names. Where are you getting your mailing list from? While I never advocate paying for a list (if you can help it) because they're pretty expensive and not always worth the money, I recommend instead a Google search for various associations (many list e-mail addresses) or if it's in your budget try purchasing a business directory like The Pride Pages(free) of Bizjournal.com (less than $100 annually) which publishes The San Francisco Book of lists which is... a list of top businesses(key employees and e-mails too).

· E-mail/direct mail. Whichever method you choose, make sure your message is compelling and clear enough to get the prospects attention (and sell tickets). Part of the reason for sluggish ticket sales might be an unclear or un-compelling message. In other words, why should I attend?

· Price-This is tricky because you should charge enough to cover overhead (while showing a profit) without pricing yourself out of the market. Will your target audience pay $200 for a cold calling seminar? Probably not. But they may pay if you include sales strategies and motivational talks. This is where you have to really crunch the numbers and evaluate the worth of the information you're bringing to the table. Want to make it easier to take payments? Set up an Eventbrite account and connect it to your Paypal account. Attendees simply click on the link and presto, you've got a payment .Eventbrite also allows you to send out invitations, manage guests lists and track your progress.

· Promote consistently and never stop promoting on Facebook, Linkedin, event websites, Twitter, e-mail and direct mail. Schedule media interviews to get the word out. Partner with others to get them to promote your work. Here's how to tell if your campaign is on the right track. If after 3 weeks you haven't sold a single ticket to your event, then it's time re-write(and re-think) your message. Here's another tip. Always allow 60-90 days to promote your event. It's rare that potential attendees buy tickets based on first contact. It usually takes 5 contacts before they do.

2.   Blogging. Yes. Blogging is still as relevant today as it was years ago when the term first made its way into the global vernacular. In fact anyone not blogging is missing out on a prime opportunity to keep their name in front of their target audience (not to mention revenue). Why? Because a well written, well promoted blog will generate advertisers as well as readers. Just ask PEREZ Hilton who has millions of readers worldwide and earns millions writing about celebrities. And let's not forget that blogs can be turned into books, workshops and consulting gigs.

3.   Internet Radio/TV shows. Here's rule #1. If you want to turn your show into a money maker, don't refer to it as a "podcast." "Internet radio show or Internet TV show" is much better and sends a message that it's a regular part of your brand instead of a hobby. It's the difference between writing a blog and writing a column. It's subtle but important because in my experience advertisers tend to spend money on columns and radio shows and not podcasts. Hosting a show of your own allows you to build your brand in a global market and reach millions.

4.   Publish or perish. Once you've produced a decent amount of material (about 6 months' worth) in your blog then it's time to compile and edit your best content into a manuscript. Keep in mind that your book needn't be any longer than 120 pages long. The point is to produce quality content packaged into book form and marketed as part of your brand.

5.   Host a networking event /group. Not happy with the networking events you're currently attending? Host one of your own. Many bars and restaurants will gladly waive the room rental costs if you can bring them say 50 new customers for an event. Hosting your own networking group allows you to invite the guests you want, network with prospects that you want to network with and promote your services to your target audience.

Chapter Thirteen: Contacts-Who's hiring?-Our list of organizations that hire speakers

We compiled the following list over the last year to give you the most up to date contact information available. Most are non-paid speaking engagements that allow speakers to make an offer. However, nearly all of the contacts are terrific opportunities for speakers to increase their e-mail lists and sell directly to workshop attendees. For a complete list be sure to visit http://joom.ag/FaGb

NAWBO Sacramento Valley
P.O. Box 189222

Sacramento, CA 95818

916-538-4249

info@nawbo-sac.org

Books speakers for both morning and evening events. As of Oct 31, 2015 they will be accepting submissions via their website only. Speakers can make an offer. Register at

http://nawbo-sac.com/speakers.html

NAWBO-San Diego
P.O. Box 880263

San Diego, CA 92168

Phone/Fax: 877.866.2926

Email: info@nawbo-sd.org

Books speakers for both morning and evening events. Submit 1 sheet

Hult International Business School*
1355 Sansome St, San Francisco, CA 94111

(415) 869-2900

Books speakers for their Career services dept. Has a budget. Send 1 sheet

Contact: Sheena.Caines@hult.edu

Wearewatermark.org

Linda Lyddon is the Director of Events and Nida Khalil is the Director of Membership for Watermark, a fabulous community of professional women at the top of their fields.

Send 1 sheet to Linda Lyddon linda@wearewatermark.org

SDD Conference

This is one of the largest Software conferences and held in London. You can speak on any subject so long as it's applicable for the industry (i.e. Leadership strategies for software development, Stress and anxiety management for Tech professionals)

http://sddconf.com/submissions/

"Change Your World" Virtual Summit

Typically happens in September. Got to http://publicspeakersassociation.com . You must be a member in order to present at the summit

Montréal-Python 54: Virtualized Utopia

For the occasion, we are looking for speakers (Everything from business to philosophy.) to give talks of 5, 10, 20, or even 45 minutes. Come tell us about your latest discoveries, your latest module, or your latest professional or personal realizations. It is your chance to meet with the local Python community.

Send us your propositions at mtlpyteam@googlegroups.com

Silicon Valley Leadership Group

The Annual Education Summit is a conference that brings together nearly 400 industry executives, education advocates, and elected officials to actively engage in meaningful discussions to strengthen our education system.

Kristina Peralta

Director of Education and Workforce

Silicon Valley Leadership Group

(408) 501-7863 | kperalta@svlg.org

ComplianceOnline.com*

Manish Kumar Singh - Business Development – ComplianceOnline

Phone: (650) 284-1690

Email: manish@complianceonline.com

Address: 2600 E. Bayshore Road, Palo Alto, CA 94303, USA

Books speakers for paid webinars and seminars. E-mail Manish for specific topics and details

US Autism & Asperger Association Speaker's Bureau

US Autism & Asperger Association offers a Speaker's Bureau that consist of many of our conference speakers that are available to present at your events or workshops. Contact us for more information about this program or call us at 1-801-816-1234. http://www.usautism.org/contact_us.htm

Indian Creek Foundation

Do you speak on subject for or to people and staff of disabilities?

We are looking for speakers in southeastern Pennsylvania who are interested in an audience made up of staff working with children and adults with intellectual and developmental disabilities. We are a small private non-profit agency located about 35 miles north of the city of Philadelphia. Topics are to be discussed and determined with each individual speaker thru me.

Indian Creek Foundation is a private, non-profit organization which has been in operation for the past 40 years. We specialize in working with persons who have intellectual as well as developmental disabilities. We serve adults, children and families in both Montgomery and Bucks County, Pennsylvania. We own and operate group homes, adult day programs, an outpatient clinic, a nursing clinic, and work with over 600 families at this time. We currently have about 270 staff, and we offer brown bag lunch programs each month for all of our staff to attend. I coordinate those outside speakers, and we attempt to offer a large variety of topics that would be of interest to our staff. We have a mix of nurses, administrative staff, as well as direct care workers here. My e-mail address and phone number are listed below, and I can respond to any messages. Because we are a non-profit foundation, we cannot offer an honorarium to any of our outside speakers.

Ted Middleburg (267) 203-1500

Ted Middleburg

Training Coordinator

Indian Creek Foundation

420 Cowpath Road

Souderton, PA 18964

ph: 267.203.1500 x 319

tmiddleburg@indcreek.org

www.indcreek.org

Public Speakers Association

Tonya Hofmann is President of the Public Speakers Association and host of the popular Tonya Hofmann Show. Tonya also e-mails regular weekly speaking opportunities to her members. However you must be a member to take advantage of these updates. To register, go to http://publicspeakersassociation.com/

Be sure to mention Tony Wilkins referred you.

New York CPA Certified Public Accountants Nassau County

http://www.st-cpas.com/ They book speakers for their conferences and monthly meetings. Send 1 sheet to Jean Townsend jtownsend@st-cpas.com

The Lean Startup Conference 2015 info@leanstartup.co

Hosts in San Francisco in Nov. Starts looking for speakers at least 1 year in advance.

PBWC's Young Women's Summit is a one of a kind event designed to inspire young women to dream big and reach high while providing them with the real-world tools they need to achieve their goals.

Annual conference is in Oct. Send 1 sheet. http://pbwc.org/event/young-womens-summit/

CIIS California Institute of Integral Studies

Laura Reddick Public Program Director 415-575-6113 Lreddick@ciis.edu

Books speakers throughout the year to speak on a variety of topics including clinical depression to business 101.

Alex Carroll - Radio Publicity Alex@RadioPublicity.com
Santa Barbara, CA 93109

Books speakers for one of the top teleseminars in the world.

San Jose Chamber of commerce
Whitney Divers   whitneyd@sjchamber.com

408-291-5250   http://www.sjchamber.com/about/chamber-staff/

Books speakers (primarily members for regular speaking engagements)

Santa Clara SBDC
408-385-9151 MIMIHNDz@SBDCHC.ORG Mimi Hernandez

100 E Santa Clara St, San Jose, CA 95113

Speaker Summit is in Oct. Looking in Aug for speakers. Speakers can make an offer.

Renaissance Center rencenter.org
April Gilbert, Program Director* makes final decision on booking speakers

agilbert@rencenter.org (415) 348-6210

Advocamp 2016 Call For Speakers Now Open**
SAN FRANCISCO, CA--(Marketwired - Oct 22, 2015) - Advocamp, the only conference to celebrate the culture of customer advocacy, is coming back to San Francisco March 7-9, 2016 and the call for speakers is now open.

The second annual Advocamp will host more than 1,000 customer-obsessed business leaders, and feature over 50 thought provoking keynotes and high energy, TED Talk-style sessions called AMP Talks. Advocamp organizers Influitive will accept applications from the best minds and biggest personalities in business until Friday, December 4, 2015.

Podium Magazine Annual- 2016 Edition

THE BIG BOOK OF EVENT PLANNERS,PROFESSIONAL
COACHES, CONSULTANTS ,SPEAKERS, & MEDIA
CONTACTS,

The essential tool for finding speaking & media opportunities
worldwide

For more contacts of meeting planners visit http://joom.ag/FaGb

Chapter Fourteen: Top ways to get paid as a speaker

Okay I have to admit it. I've become a bit of a grump in my old age. Booking speakers for engagements will sometimes do that to you. Repeating yourself to deaf ears will also cause a normally patient person to lose it on occasion. Part of what makes me an effective speaker, lecturer and booker of speakers is that I've been there and done that. I've spoken to a room of 200+ and to rooms of just 2 people. I've had people respond favorably to my work and not so much. I've also spoken with decision makers that book speakers; speakers that command thousands in speaking fees and attendees of speaking events. Bottom line? I know what works and what doesn't when it comes to booking speaking engagements. So I decided to offer my top tips for speakers that every speaker should live by.....

1.   Speak about what you know but be able to speak about multiple topics as well. Speaking is like writing. Writers write about what they know, but they also write about things they're not necessarily experts on. Meaning that if someone is willing to pay them well about a subject they aren't familiar with, you can be sure they are going to do their research and come up with piece worthy of getting paid to write. It's essentially the same with actors. Actors are told that if an agent approaches them with a plumb role that requires them to do something they aren't familiar with doing (like driving or riding a bike) they say "yes, I can do that" and figure the rest out later. Speaking professionally has the same rules (in my opinion). Many speakers only talk on one topic but and then wonder why they aren't booking more engagements. The truth is that decision makers look for speakers that can talk both well and on a number of subjects. Look at it this way. Event planners get calls on a daily basis from speakers all vying for that 1 spot at the upcoming conference. What sets you apart from them? And what if they've already booked a similar for that conference? What will you do now? If you're smart you'll list a number of topics on your one sheet. I'm not saying not to speak on your area of expertise but you'll stand a better chance of getting booked if you have more arrows in your quiver.

2.   Have a one sheet ready to go. What's amazing to me is the number of speakers that don't even know what a one sheet is and why it's important. And truth be told, until the last several years I was one of them. Now it's important to note that I booked a lot of speaking engagements (coaching sessions mostly) on without one and did very well doing it too. But what I soon realized was that to get the big speaking gigs, the $5000 per speech gigs required a decent one sheet. Again it's like booking an acting gig; you can book all of the regional theater gigs you want. But to book the bigger gigs that pay, you need a resume that sells (which is all a one sheets is).

3.   Connect with your audience. Many speakers I talk to simply go into a speaking gig with the intention of " making an offer" or closing the deal. And there's nothing wrong with that; after all, that's

why we speak. However, if you really want to make money, then you must connect with your audience in order to sell them on your product or service otherwise you're just selling them something without substance.

4.   Learn to make money, even when you're speaking for free. I have a rule. While I don't accept every speaking gig that comes my way, I do try and see the business opportunities from speaking in front of a specific group. As I told one of my booking clients, I never worry about making money by speaking pro bono because I always do. That is to say that when I speak for free I always make sure I have contact info for attendees. This allows me to send them info on other products and services which usually translates into sales.

5.   Book a mixture of pro bono, paid and media engagements ;particularly if you're just starting out or if your name isn't as established as say a Tony Robbins. Booking all 3 will go a long way to building your brand. Speakers that only try and book paid speaking engagements are missing out. You can book all of the paid speaking engagements you want. But if no one knows who you are then you'll be hard pressed to take you speaking business to the next level. That's why a combo of the 3 are always best. Once you've established yourself then you can pick and choose where you speak.

More tips
Top ways to get paid for speaking

1.   The fastest way to get paid to speak is to hire yourself. There are 2 key ways to make this work. The first is to get paid before you speak and the second is to get paid after you speak as a consultant. Here's how you do it….

A.   To get paid before you speak is fairly simple. You need a subject and an audience and a location. Determine who it is that you want to speak to. Is this a subject they will find interesting. Why? Do you have an e-mail list to send invitations? What e-mail marketing tool will you use to get their attention? How will you track your progress? If you're charging make sure it's enough to cover your costs for room rental, food etc. Don't make the mistake of spending $1400 on a workshop (which is what one of my clients did) only to find that no one is interested in signing up. Also give yourself enough time to market and tweak any issues. I 'd say about 90 days for marketing any event is a safe bet because you want to give yourself enough time to get the word out. You also want to determine how many signups you need to start making money. If it takes more than 3 then either you better have a dynamite talk that everyone wants to come to or you need to charge more and have fewer people. Use Eventbrite to promote and collect ticket sales and be sure to have a Paypal account set up so that sales can go directly into your account. There's nothing better than seeing "You've got cash" in your in box. If you have a book, dvd or other product to sell, this is the time to promote it. When I began my speaking career I promoted my books as well as my consulting services which always garnered sales after the talk.

B.   To get paid after the talk

There are several reasons speakers talk for free. First, it's great exposure and usually the facilitators handle all of the marketing and promotion for free. You will most likely get a decent audience (about 25 plus is a good audience). And it's easier to get a non-paid speaking gig than a paid gig and any opportunity to get in front of your targeted audience. Now, if you offer a free webinar or workshop you're almost guaranteed a good audience which means lots of e-mails and contact information. The way to make money from it is to make sure you have products and services in place to sell after the talk. This includes DVD and book sales, consulting and coaching contracts and any other services you'd like to sell. The more products and options you have to offer the better.

C.   Launch your own podcast/Internet TV show and make money via advertising

D.   Get large corporations to sponsor an event with you as a speaker

E.   Get placed on a panel of experts

F.   Write a book that speaks directly to other speakers

G.   Create a workshop or product that speaks directly to speakers

Chapter Fifteen: Where and how to find speaking gigs

One of the many problems speakers run into is finding speaking gigs as well as knowing where to look. The following are some of my top tips for booking your next speaking opportunity.

1.   "Am I in the right market?" This should be one of the first questions speakers should ask themselves when trying to book jobs. For example, are you motivational speaker, a sales coach, a life coach or a key note speaker? Who's your market? In other words, who would you like to hear your message and why should they hear you speak? Do your research to determine how well received the topic will be by your audience and how much revenue you can generate from the industry based on the subject matter.

2.   Don't make the topic fit the market. Instead speak to a specific market and decide which topics to speak on.

3.   What can the market bear and is it worth your asking price? Leadership topics tend to be more aligned with corporations and even mid-size firms hire leadership coaches. For example, if you're a keynote speaker with a fee of $10,000 for a 90 minute speech you'll most likely get paid your regular rate if you contact decision makers of larger corporations. But companies with less than 10 employees

aren't generally interested in leadership issues-at least not initially and thus not likely to pay such a high premium.

4.   Do your homework. What are similar speakers charging? You may not be ready to charge a similar amount but you can get close. And speaking of which….

5.   Ask for what you want and be clear about it. No haggling. You're not running a non- profit. If your fee is $3000 then make sure you state it with conviction. If you appear (to the decision) to be unsure of your fees then you can be sure that they won't be willing to pay you what you're worth. And while haggling over price shows that you're willing to negotiate down (not always a good thing) it's okay to negotiate a deal you're comfortable with. If you find yourself doing this a lot then you're selling to the wrong market. It's really about valuing your worth and not settling.

6.   Want more speaking gigs? Engage the audience. Every expert I interviewed made the same point. If the audience isn't connecting with you as a speaker, then why should you be invited back? And why should they refer you? Professional speaking is about connecting with the audience on a real level. It's about authenticity. If you're not authentic, the audience will know it immediately and be turned off.

7.   Ask for referrals after the speaking engagement. If you've given a commanding lecture, make sure you do the following: 1. Video the tape and upload it to your site. After all this is how speakers get hired. 2. Ask the decision maker for referrals of other contacts who might be interested in hiring you. 3. Ask for testimonials. If you've given a great talk they shouldn't have a problem singing your praises.

8.   Look to the corporate sector for speaking gigs. I'm not sure why but for some reason I lingered far too long in the small business market which pays well and often but not as well as mid and large market gigs. Bottom line-look to other markets or struggle as a speaker. Trust me; I know a lot of great speakers that aren't making nearly the amount they could be making. Don't underestimate your potential.

9.   Marketing is important. Make sure your message is clear. Why are attendees expected to attend? Is this a free event or is there a fee? If there is a fee, is it worth the price? How many are you expecting to attend? Who is your market? What will attendees receive in the way of information for attending? Make sure to tell attendees why they should attend.

10.   Make it worth their while. There is nothing more disappointing than attending an event (even a free one) only to walk away feeling like it was a waste of time (which is even more of a sin than wasting someone's money). Be willing to ask after every talk if the attendees got anything out of the session. If they can name one important piece of info they garnered from attending then you've done your job.

11.   Document the experience. One mistake I made early in my career was not documenting all of my talks. "Speaker reels" are just one way speakers get the attention of meeting planners. It's important that decision makers can see you in action. Even for 5 min. Trust me, it makes a difference. Why should anyone hire you if they've never heard or seen you speak?

12.   Create a sense of urgency- Let's face it. Most business owners would rather do just about anything else other than attend a workshop. The trick to getting your attendance up at any event is creating a sense of urgency as well as a real purpose for attending. Why should they attend? What will they get out of it'? Is it worth it to buy tickets early or wait till a few days before the event? What's the payoff for buying tickets early? Is there a discount? Make sure you're giving attendees a purpose for attending not to mention a reason for buying early.

13.   What to charge? There was a time early in my career when charging a few hundred an hour was a big deal for a speaking engagement. That notion was immediately dismissed when interviewing a group of professional speakers about how they determine their rates. The consensus is this. Depending on your market (corporate speaker, coach, keynote etc.) decision makers won't take a speaker that charges less than $2500 for a 90 minute keynote speech seriously. In this same group there was a heated debate as to whether or not to haggle over speaker rates. Half of the group felt that haggling was demeaning and undervalues the speaker's abilities and expertise. "Set your rate and stick to it". While the other group felt that a little maneuverability is always preferable, particularly if you're trying to close the deal. It dawned on me that this really has to do with perception as well as how badly one wants the account. In other words, if you're like most of us and can't afford to walk away from the negotiating table, you'll most likely haggle a bit over your rates. Not so much that you undervalue your work but enough to be able to close the deal within the client's budget. However if you're a more sought after (high end)speaker who isn't hurting for speaking opportunities then you might feel comfortable stating your rate and walking away if the prospect can't meet it. So which group is right? In my opinion both. Again, walking away from the table is a good idea only if you can afford to do it or the perception is that you can afford to do it. It shows that you don't need the money. On the other hand you should be charging enough to ensure that you don't have to hustle for work. Here's the other side of the coin and a powerful lesson that I learned awhile back. If you feel that you're not charging enough and that the prospects you're engaging aren't willing to pay your rate; then you're probably going after the wrong market. Remember when I was happily going after $200 an hour clientele? I really wanted to kick my speaking career up to the next level but didn't know how to go about it. And then it dawned on me that if I want to get paid more for my work then I would need to not only charge more but charge the right clientele more for my services. That meant going after prospects that could afford to pay a premium for my work (after 30+ years as a business development consultant I think I'm worth at least that much). So while I still consult small business owners my hourly rate has increased to $375 an hour and I have a speaking rate of $7500 for a 90 min keynote speech (working up to $10,000). Of course I can only charge that because my clientele are organizations that can afford it.

14.   So who's hiring? Here's a list of industries that hire speakers on a regular basis. If you're like most speakers you're always on the lookout for opportunities to showcase your expertise. Here's a list of suggestions whether you're a seasoned speaker or just getting started....'

A.   Churches- While not all churches are willing to pay a premium for speakers, most are willing to pay a small honorarium to attract speakers who can connect with their congregation on topics important to parishioners.

B.   Women's conferences ,groups and trade shows-Women's issues are really important these days and while most prefer female speakers you can tailor your talk to a more female –centric audience even if you're a man. Trade shows are always looking for top speakers to attract business owners so make sure to connect with the facilitators of these shows.

C.   Corporations-Which sounds like a no brainer I know and to be frank, corporations are the holy grail of speaking "gets". They pay more and better than say" Joes Auto "and are happy to shell out extra for amenities like travel expenses.

D.   Nonprofits-Surprising enough, the larger nonprofits have funds that are allocated for speakers and are fine with paying a premium for speakers

E.   Trade Associations- These are the top tiered speaking gigs. Harder to get but once you do (and provided you do a great job) can pay HUGE dividends-including referrals.

F.   American Society of Associations/State Associations-For every organization out there; there's probably an association associated with the organization. Do a bit of research to find the one that's applicable to your subject matter. Again these are not for the unseasoned speaker; you've got to work up to these.

G.   Make connections to religious leaders, HR Directors, Event planners and office managers for bookings.

H.   Colleges, Government agencies and universities and high schools. These like churches tend to be a bit easier in terms of booking speaking engagements because they're usually hungry to have experts come in and educate their constituents.

I.   SBA, Learning Annex, Small Business Development Centers- Let's take these one at a time. The Small Business Administration (SBA) was the very first professional speaking gig I ever did (many years ago) and while they don't pay their speakers, the exposure you get is priceless-particularly if you get in front of 50 or more eager to learn attendees. Learning Annex-yes that Learning Annex offers classes of virtually every subject. And while they take a percentage of all sales they also handle all the promotion which means you're almost guaranteed an audience. Small Business Development Centers-These are the sister offices to the SBA. And while they don't get as much funding, or press as most business organizations, there is still a need for speakers. Usually there is no per diem but again the exposure is terrific.

J.   Libraries- Did you know that most libraries have a budget to hire speakers? It's not a lot, perhaps under $1000 per speaker but still it's more about the exposure than the big dollars. Perfect for newer speakers and speakers that want to test a new topic presentation.

15.   Make a connection with your audience-People are intuitive. They can tell when you're insincere or inauthentic. The best speakers are the ones that connect with their audience. I think what makes me an excellent speaker is the fact that I work with every attendee on a one on one basis. My goals are always to help educate and listen to the stories of everyone attending one of my sessions.

16.   Speak in front of everyone until you build your brand- Most speakers are always on the hunt for a great speaking opportunity. If it's a paid opportunity all the better; but some of the best opportunities come without any initial pay. Organizations like the Small Business Administration book speakers that can deliver a quality talk without promoting anything. However, if you are lucky enough to book an engagement with your local SBA take advantage of it because a good talk will always garner the respect and attention of the attendees; most of whom are only too happy to offer you their business card after the talk. And this is your opportunity to send them info on your other services, turning them into paying clients. Be careful however that in your exuberance to get in front of an audience that you don't sacrifice your chance to earn a paycheck just to get in front of an audience. If you do speak "for free" be sure to remember these tips .

A. Only accept pro bono engagements if you're likely to turn them into paying clients later.

B. Only accept pro bono engagements if you're just starting out as a speaker.

C. Only accept pro bono engagements if you can sell products/services during or immediately after the talk.

D. Only accept pro bono engagements if it helps build your brand, particularly by partnering with a much more established brand.

E. Only accept pro bono engagements if the organization hosting it will promote it and fill seats.

F. Only accept pro bono engagements if it's hosted by an organization or institution you support (i.e. a small nonprofit)

G. Remember it's only pro bono or "free speaking" if you don't generate another speaking gig from the first one you don't add to your e-mail list or you can't convert attendees into paying customers. Otherwise you are speaking for free.

17.   Expand your speaking range to include subjects a bit out of your comfort zone. When I began my career as a speaker I only taught cold calling workshops. But as my experience grew so did my range in topics. Now my topics range from cold calling to career advancement to marketing/sales strategies to leadership and motivation.

18.   Be consistent with your marketing efforts. Nothing can kill a marketing campaign like the lack of consistency. Be sure to send e-mail blasts and promote via social media several times a week to keep your name in front of your target audience.

19.   Make sure your message is clear. In your need to get your message in front of others, you may neglect the most important aspect for a good marketing campaign-clarity. Why should people attend your talk? What will they get out of it? Make sure your message is about what they will get by attending and not about selling your event. Give them a reason to buy tickets.

20.   Create a speaker reel of yourself- If you're new to speaking, your 3 most important tools for landing speaking gigs is your one sheet (which describes who you are and what your specialty is) a short video of you speaking and a website. Having this in your arsenal shows decision makers that you're a professional and not a novice.

21.   Ask for testimonials and referrals. Testimonials and referrals go a long way to establish credibility. Make sure you're also endorsed on Linkedin which again establishes credibility. Referrals are another way to land more gigs, so don't forget to ask for them.

22.   How do I make contact? The key to making contact is to first decide where you want to speak*. See our list of places to speak. Next, pull together a list of organizations to call. What you want to know is the name of the meeting planner. How often they bool speakers. The type of speakers and topics they book. Are the speakers paid? And if so, how much (ask about their budget)? Next send your one sheet and be sure to follow up a week later. Following up is the single most important element to booking more speaking engagements.

Want to ensure a great audience? Remember these rules.

A.   Prep-Do your research. What subjects are most important to your audience? How can you make your subject matter relevant?

B.   Position yourself so that you become the "go to person" in your industry for great talks.

C.   Make sure your talk has a great title. This means it has to grab the attention of potential attendees and make them want to buy tickets.

D.   Be clear about why they should attend your event. If your message isn't clear and concise how can you expect anyone to show up? More importantly make your message about how you can help attendees and what they'll get when attending.

E.   Ask for your fee and for the engagement. It's one of the first rules in sales. Ask for the sale which sounds simplistic but you'd be amazed at the number of speakers that don't ask.

F.   Partner with an organization that can help bring in attendees. If you're an unknown speaker one task to undertake is building a database of decision makers who work for brands that are already established but are looking for joint pr.

G.   Speaking opportunities are all around you. On Facebook, Twitter, hotels and convention centers. But how often do you walk into a hotel and ask the concierge about upcoming events? Let's take it one step further. How often do you write down the name of the conference and other contact info necessary for bookings? Is the event an annual event? Is it an event for women? Business owners? Is it a national event? Once you capture the info make sure you keep it on a spreadsheet or database so you can follow up months in advance. This ensures that you NEVER run out of speaking opportunities.

Chapter Sixteen: Here are the top reasons you're not booking more speaking engagements and how to turn that around once and for all.

I recently had a chat with one of my clients; a lovely woman who is a terrific speaker and coach. She had been struggling to book more speaking gigs for herself but found it extremely difficult (even with my help). Now in order to truly understand the issue, I must point out a few facts....

1.   As a booker I don't negotiate rates for my speakers. Rates are usually on the one sheet of the speakers.

2.   I send one sheets to the target audience of the speaker, follow up with a phone call and then book the gig.

3.   In order for a successful booking to occur, the event planner must....

A.   Have a need to book the speaker. In other words bookings are a priority.

B.   Have a budget to pay the speaker unless it will be a pro bono engagement and the speaker can make an offer.

If these components are not in place then there is no booking. The most important component of course is that the planner must have a need to book a speaker.

Decision makers receive hundreds if not thousands of requests per year; so many in fact that many organizations usually have a special portal on their website just for submissions. So when my client came to me with this dilemma I looked at what was really going on with her. Turns out she was making some serious mistakes in trying to get bookings. So here's what I told her...

1.   First she had a topic that would only be of interest to a very specific audience (stress and anxiety); which means that the majority of business organizations wouldn't have an interest in booking her unless it was applicable to business people. So my advice was to make her topic more applicable to the business community. By tweaking her topic for a new target audience (every day people as well as business owners) she broadens her audience as well as ensures that the people she's speaking to can actually afford her services. It is one thing to talk to someone making $20 an hour with anxiety issues (who may only hire her for a few sessions) but it's a whole new ball game to speak to business owners that might be able to afford her services long term. Both are important but the second will generate more long term revenue and opportunities. The point is to speak in front of people who can actually afford to hire you.

2.   Second she had to change her one sheet to include multiple topics to increase her visibility. To be honest she still fights me on this one but I put it to her this way. Every speaker I rep speak on multiple topics because they realize they aren't at the level of a Jeff Hayzlett or a Tony Robbins. That means that in order to land more gigs, they must cast a wider net. It is one thing to have a signature talk when you're at that level it's quite another when you're trying to get to that level.

3.   Here's an example. An event planner contacted me about booking some speakers for $1000 a day plus travel and food. The topics were varied and I suggested she speak on a topic that most speakers can speak to-project management. Yes it would require that she perhaps research the topic and develop some top tips; but what speaker can't talk about project management for $1000 a day? Again she fought me tooth and nail and eventually turned the deal down.

4.   She must pick up the phone. Okay, truth be told everyone hates this aspect of marketing and sales but it's necessary. Even if you hire someone to make calls for you no one can represent you better than you can yourself. Keep in mind that as a business owner you'll want to keep tabs on what's trending in the industry; which means that you'll have to ask questions and make calls to the event planners who are booking speakers. It is fine to hire someone to make calls but it's even better if you can roll up your sleeves and book some engagements on your own. It will also give you a better perception of what a booker or agent goes thru to book gigs.

5.   She must work the leads already in her database as well as leads that are sent to her. What often surprises me are the number of speakers that have leads just sitting in their database for years without any follow up. Nearly every business owner I know has this problem because lead generation isn't an instinctive part of their repertoire. For most business owners it's about the next new lead rather than what's already in their database.

6.   She must utilize resources like speaker groups at her disposal to land gigs. We all have opportunities that come our way on a regular basis whether it's meeting key people or joining groups that can support us. But the real trick is to work the resources at your disposal to get to the next level. So think about all of the people that you know. Who in your circle can help you with introductions, speaking opportunities etc.? And are you utilizing those contacts effectively.

7.   She must partner with other speakers to gain exposure. Sometimes pooling your resources is the best way to go when you're building a brand. If no one knows who you are it makes sense to partner with a more established speaker to gain an audience.

8.   Busy work isn't the same as running a business. This is a big issue with many speakers who are also business owners. They get so focused on shuffling papers that they forget that in order to run a business effectively and efficiently, they must close deals. In fact, closing deals should be in your top 5 daily tasks. This was the major flaw in her overall plan

9.   Stop making excuses. Get it done. One of my pet peeves is the fact that some business owners will give you every excuse in the book for not bringing in any more business. Again it boils down to "busy work" as opposed to running a business.

10.   Tell others that you want more gigs. One of my best weapons for booking gigs is to tell others that I want more speaking gigs. When others know what you want, they can help you get to the right people;which she had a problem with; which brings me to my final point....

11.   Give to get. Whenever I meet new people I always ask 2 questions. What do you need and how can I help? Asking these two questions has opened more doors for me than just about any other marketing tool in my arsenal.

Chapter Seventeen: Speaking at the SBA and Small Business Week

So every year I receive a number of requests from the SBA(Small Business Administration) asking me to either teach a regular class from cold calling to making money as a speaker. I also receive queries to teaching during SBW (Small Business Week) which is also hosted in part by the SBA. So I thought I would offer some tips and observations for landing speaking engagements for both. Since each are marketed and booked differently I've separated these two tips into 2 lists.

SBA.GOV

1.   Bring plenty of business cards. In fact, order them at least 30 days before you need them. Since SBA speaking engagements happen throughout the year, I tend to keep at least 250 cards on hand at all times and go for high quality/low cost options like www.vistaprint.com .

2.   When contacting the SBA, ask to speak with the person responsible for booking speakers. If they try to transfer you to SCORE, which connects business leaders with people looking for mentors, be sure to state that you're interested in teaching a workshop. Teaching a workshop and mentoring are in fact two different things. The key here is to establish a relationship with the SBA so that they can contact you to teach classes on a regular basis which gives you massive exposure.

3.   Don't sell anything. Have you ever attended a workshop where you know it's a sales pitch the minute the speaker steps on stage? These types of workshops are an immediate turn off for attendees and promoters for the most part and yet many high level speakers maker millions off of the type of workshops that start out as sales pitch. "Making an offer" at the end of a talk is not the same thing as giving a 90 minute infomercial like pitch. Neither is allowable at the SBA however you can exchange business cards after the talk.

4.   SBA handles all of the marketing. It's true. The SBA handles e-mailing their extensive list of contacts. However the best way to utilize the SBA is to invite your target audience to attend (these are the people that can actually afford to hire you). Let's say you've been trying to get a meeting planner to hire you as a speaker. Why not send them an invitation to attend your free workshop at the SBA. They get to see you in action first hand and if they like what they see, may hire you for another speaking gig. Be sure to collect (discretely) business cards of all attendees

5.   There is no upfront pay. The SBA doesn't pay their speakers and generally frowns on speakers promoting their services at workshops. You may have business cards on hand but be careful not to sell any products. The way to make money is to simply ask attendees after the event how you can help them, exchange business cards and most importantly-follow up with an e-mail and a phone call

6.   There are several reasons to teach at the SBA.

A.   You want to try out a new workshop to see if you can turn it into a book, series of paying workshop etc.

B.   You want to give back to the community.

C.   You're looking for a platform to teach.

7.   Want to make money after speaking at the SBA? Pick up the phone after you teach. I cannot stress this enough. Many speakers will send an e-mail to attendees but can't be bothered to see if any attendees received your e-mail or how you can help them. Keep in mind, these attendees came to learn what you know and if you're smart you'll give them just enough to establish yourself as an expert without giving away the farm.

8.   Handouts are good because they allow attendees to remember tips, which is why I never have them at my workshops. I know that sounds odd but here's the thing about handouts. If an attendee has a handout with all of your tips then why should they call you afterwards?

9.   Expect approx. 20-30 attendees per workshop. The SBA will generally get 40+ people to RSVP for any given workshop; however the prospects that actually attend are roughly about ½ which is considered a good class by their standards(mine too).

10.   SBA is not for speakers that make $10,000+ per speech. If you're making this much money per speech I would say teaching via the SBA might not be for you. It's really for those speakers that want to build a brand or develop a new market. If you're able to command more than $10,000 per speech your brand is pretty much developed.

11.   You can speak at multiple SBA offices in multiple cities. While the SBA cannot endorse you directly, they can (and will) send you feedback from attendees, which you can then parlay into other speaking gigs.

Small Business Week

Teaching during Small Business Week is similar to teaching at SBA just on a larger scale. It's one of the best opportunities for speakers and if you're lucky enough to get picked to speak (it's can be a gold mine). Here's what you need to know about SBW in order to get the most out of it.

1.   Sign up early. SBW in SF typically takes place the second week in May. So I start connecting with organizers in March (Late Feb is even better). SBW is sponsored in part by the SBA which means the same rules apply when it comes to promoting (or rather not promoting) yourself to attendees. Banks, professional organizations also play an important role in the planning and execution of this event which means there's a great opportunity to network with organizers to try and get booked for other events.

2.   The person to contact for Adam Straus of Strauss Events http://strausevents.com/ Adam an amazingly busy guy, is usually good about getting back to everyone he's interested in booking a few weeks before the event.

3.   The SBW handles all of the promotion for you. Here's where it gets interesting. While speaking at the SBA might net you anywhere from 10-30 attendees per workshop, the SBW will generally net you at least 40 and up to 100. And because Straus Events handles the promotion you're almost guaranteed a good turnout for your talk.

4.   You get all this and the e-mail list of attendees. This is the part I get most excited about. First, to teach a class with over 40 people without having to promote it is terrific. However to get an Excel spreadsheet with contacts (including e-mails) makes this a gold mine of an opportunity. Now in case it's not obvious to you, there are several ways to generate revenue from this list. First, make sure you send an invitation (to hear you speak) to your target audience. Just because you don't need to do any promotion for the event doesn't mean you can't pepper the audience with people that might hire you as a consultant. Second, after you've taught your class, be sure to send an e-mail to attendees thanking them for attending. Be sure to include a link to your site and any products/services you'd like to promote. I tend to trade lists with my clients (who I've booked for SBW) as a way of increasing both my list as well as theirs. This year I quadrupled my list to nearly 200 contacts. The one question to ask is "how can I help you?"

5.   Your name and company is instantly promoted. Having your name on the SBW site is a great way to earn instant credibility. And best of all any time someone searching for info on you will see that you were a featured speaker at the event.

6.   There is no excuse for not closing any deals after a speaking event. These prospects came to hear you speak. So why wouldn't you let them know about other products and services.

Chapter Eighteen: 5 ways to create lucrative partnerships that fill seats and generate revenue

For me, creating any partnership is not just about choosing the right partners for a project but about choosing people or organizations that enhance your brand. Here's a list of ways to create better partnerships that generate money.

1.Partnerships will rarely be 50-50. Meaning that you may wind up doing most of the work which is fine so long as you're getting more visibility, money or contacts out of the deal. So while you may be handling most of the grunt work (advertising-mail marketing etc.) if you're getting what you need out of it the arrangement, just smile and keep cultivating the relationship.

2.Partner with a larger, more established organization that will give you more visibility, credibility and brand awareness. For example; two of my biggest partnerships (with my radio show) include Le Cordon Blu and The Payne Mansion. Why was it important to partner with these two organizations? Simple. Brand awareness. Many business owners know about my show but by partnering with a worldwide award winning cooking school I now have international cache' . And who wouldn't want to come visit my studio at The Payne Mansion.

3.Be indispensable to your partner. I recently had a conversation with one of my partners who expressed his gratitude in being introduced to several of my high profile business contacts-many of whom are now his clients. I think it's safe to say that we'll be working together for quite some time.

4. Look for ways to extend partnerships that work. Sometimes the best partnerships are the ones that are initially intended to be short term but still work well. In those cases it's a good idea to look at ways to continue your association. To do that, be ready to renegotiate your current arrangement while asking for more (reasonable) perks. If they're really happy with the arrangement, you won't have too much trouble getting exactly what you want.

5.Replicate your partnership with similar or organization or firms that compliment your current arrangement. As long as it's not a conflict of interest with your primary partner you should be just fine

What I learned from hosting The Empowerment Conference

Sometimes you're too stupid to know what you don't know. When I came up with the idea to host the Empowerment Conference in San Francisco, I had no idea that it would be so labor intensive; which was so exhilarating and yet so incredibly frustrating. My journey as with all of my events always begins several months before the actual event. I always give myself approx. 90 days to plan and promote any event. However this was the first time I would host an event for more than a few hours. This meant my stamina and planning had to flawless. Best laid plans....

1.   Plan early. As I mentioned the more time you have to plan any event particularly a large event-the better. Give yourself a minimum of 90 days to plan and execute the event to ensure a decent turn out. You also need to give yourself breathing room just in case anything goes wrong and something always goes wrong.

2.   Get others to help you promote your event. This is where strategic partnerships come in handy. All of those people who've asked for favors over the years? Time to call in those chips because you can't do everything yourself and so it's a good idea to ask for help. Ask each person to help with things like e-mailing contacts, set up, securing caterers etc. Even having someone on hand to greet attendees and take door payments can be a great relief.

3.   Plan. Verify. Re-work-Things will always go wrong even when planning an event. There's very little you can do about it except accept it. Verifying and confirming contacts will also go a long way toward avoiding conflicts. And don't rely on a simple phone call to confirm that caterers will show up, get it in writing especially if you're getting people to donate services pro bono. That way if there are issues you can refer back to the e-mail. And if some aspect of your plan doesn't work, re-work it and move on.

4.   Make sure to have multiple speakers contribute to the conference. Try and get as many diverse speakers on the roster as possible so that there's a workshop for nearly everyone. Make sure these speakers can deliver on getting attendees. There's nothing worse than booking speakers who have no idea how to sell tickets or fill seats. Admittedly this can be very challenging, particularly if you don't have a huge following but if you have 5 people on any ticket to speak, everyone should be able to get a minimum of 5-10 people to show up. That's not a lot but you'd be amazed at how difficult it is for some speakers to come up with those numbers. It's at this point that you might have to hand hold a bit which is fine if you're up for it.

5.   Invite people you want to do business with who can benefit from attending. And this might seem like a no brainer but more inexperienced speakers might not understand that you really do have to target your marketing efforts to your audience both geographically and by level of likely interest. There's nothing worse than inviting people who are not your core audience nor are they willing to travel more than a few miles to attend your conference.

6.   Whenever possible partner with a larger more well established entity like Wells Fargo to help get the word out and fill seats. It's been my experience that doing so almost always guarantees an audience. For example, one of my partners is Payne Mansion Hotel www.paynehotel.com which allows

me to host a variety of events and offers a very prestigious atmosphere (who doesn't want to come to a mansion?) for hosting any event.

7.   Have giveaways whenever possible. I partnered with several local businesses that were interested in getting the word out about their product. I gave them all tables with the promise of exposure in one of my publications provided they e-mailed their target audience and invited them to attend the event.

8.   If at all possible partner with wineries and caterers to supply food and beverages. Sometimes they will barter services for exposure. In my case I was able to offer ads in my magazines to some (not all) of the food vendors in exchange for providing samples of their food.

9.   Charge whenever possible. There's always cost involved in hosting an event. Whether it's marketing, printing, clean up, set up or hired help. Do not fool yourself into thinking you can barter everything and not have to pay for anything. Think of it this way; if something gets broken and needs to be replaced, who's going to pay for it?

10.   The bottom line is that hosting a big event takes time and energy and co-operation by all parties. But to host a really great event? You must have exceptional partners that are willing to take your event to the next level.

Final Thoughts

I hope this book has given you a bit more insight into how to make a living as a speaker. As you can see there isn't just one way to make money but multiple ways whether it's by launching an Internet radio show or by becoming a coach or keynote speaker. Whatever you decide, the goal is pretty much the same. Make sure your voice is heard and get others to pay you to share what you know

Good Luck

Tony Wilkins

Chapter Nineteen: Resources and other stuff

Directories to check out

Note: This list represents all titles currently available in Gale Directory Library. Your library may not subscribe to all titles.

http://find.galegroup.com/gdl/help/GDLeDirListHelp.html

American Wholesalers and Distributors Directory (AWDD)

Awards, Honors & Prizes (AHP)

Brands and Their Companies (BTC)

Business Rankings Annual (BRA)

Carroll Publishing Directories: County Directory, Federal Directory, Municipal Directory, and State Directory

Consultants & Consulting Organizations Directory (CCOD)

Directories in Print (DIP)

Directory of Special Libraries and Information Centers (DSL)

Encyclopedia of American Religions (EAR)

Encyclopedia of Associations: International Organizations (IO)

Encyclopedia of Associations: National Organizations of the U.S. (EA)

Encyclopedia of Associations: Regional, State and Local Organizations (RSL)

Encyclopedia of Business Information Sources (EBIS)

Encyclopedia of Governmental Advisory Organizations (EGAO)

Gale Directory of Databases (GDD)

Here are some tips from the experts....

Have an Easy YES Offer!

When you're speaking or free as a marketing strategy, make sure you have an offer that is super easy and a no-brainer for people to want and sign up for. That could mean that you throw a bunch of bonuses into the package or you highly discount whatever it is that you're selling but only for today. Easy YES Offers that I've found work best is:

1. For an audience that hasn't paid to be there, meaning it's a free event for them, give them a complimentary strategy session with you one-on-one or a paid offer of something under $100.

2. For an audience that has paid to be there, you can do what I mentioned above and kill it, or you can do up to maybe $200 or $300 but the value has to be in the thousands and a huge deal.

I share how to do this and help you create YOUR Easy YES Offer at all of my live events and in my coaching programs. Find out more about those by getting on my email list and get a Free Gift while you're there at www.KatrinaSawa.com!

Katrina Sawa, The Jumpstart Your Biz Coach, Speaker & Author of the book, Love Yourself Successful

"Helping You Get More LOVE In Your Life & MONEY In Your Business!"

Guarantee that You Get the Gig- Use Meaningful Data

Organizations, like people, appreciate being seen and acknowledged. Hire a virtual assistant to fully research your target client's struggles and goals. Upwork is a good place to start your search. You'll know just what to say to spark their interest while demonstrating your professionalism.

Dina Lynch Eisenberg, JD

Outsourcing Strategist

http://OutsourceEasier.com

Know your subject

"Make sure you know your subject so well that you never need to speak from notes or written remarks." This completely changed how I speak in public from giving speeches to passionately speaking

Mark Sackett http://theartofactivenetworking.com/

Special thanks to....

Tonya Hofmann: www.TonyaHofmann.com, www.PublicSpeakersAssociation.com & www.SimplyFollowUp.com

Dina Lynch Eisenberg, JD

Outsourcing Strategist

http://OutsourceEasier.com

Katrina Sawa, The Jumpstart Your Biz Coach, Speaker & Author of the book, Love Yourself Successful

"Helping You Get More LOVE In Your Life & MONEY In Your Business!" www.KatrinaSawa.com

Mark Sackett http://theartofactivenetworking.com/

Barney Kramer, President/CEO

Strategic Management, LLC

www.smra1.com

Books and Resources from Tony Wilkins

All books by Tony Wilkins available at Amazon.com

Subscribe to all of our magazines or learn more about my workshops and speaking services and events at **awil267487@aol.com**

Be sure to tune in to Small Business Forum Radio at www.blogtalkradio.com/tonywilkins

SBFM   Feb. 2016

Small Business Forum Magazine

Celebrating

Black History Month

Foodie Quarterly (FQ)

The Holiday Issue
Recipes, shortcuts and everything you need for a
stress free holiday season

Seasons Greetings

Podium Monthly Magazine Jan . 2016

Meet the Fabulous Tonya Hofmann
Founder of The Public Speaker's Association

www.ingramcontent.com/pod-product-compliance
Lightning Source LLC
Chambersburg PA
CBHW051342170526
45166CB00002B/917